COMPETENCY-BASED MUSIC EDUCATION

CLIFFORD K. MADSEN
Florida State University

CORNELIA YARBROUGH
Syracuse University

CPC **CONTEMPORARY PUBLISHING COMPANY**
508 ST. MARY'S STREET, RALEIGH, N.C. 27605—(919) 821-4566

Library of Congress Cataloging in Publication Data

Madsen, Clifford K.
    Competency-based music education.

    Bibliography: p. 161
    1. School music—Instruction and study.
I. Yarbrough, Cornelia, joint author.
II. Title.
MT1.M127   780'.72   79-19265

ISBN 0-89892-061-2

Printed in the United States of America

COMPETENCY-BASED
MUSIC EDUCATION

Contents

Preface

The purpose of this book is to provide competency-based observation and field experiences for music educators whether they be student teachers, graduate music education majors, or professional music educators who teach in public or private schools, colleges, and universities. No attempt has been made to set specific competency levels in each area because it is the belief of the authors that these levels must be established and developed according to individual needs as well as the specific teaching situation, i.e., urban, rural, rehearsal, general music, elementary, secondary, and so forth. Instead, data-based techniques for the improvement of teaching and learning have been outlined.

Each chapter begins with an essay which is followed by a set of field experiences. All of the suggested field experiences concern the transfer of individual and community values to overt teaching and learning behaviors. Habits of record keeping are emphasized, for it is only when teachers realize what they have accomplished professionally, and what their present professional status is, that they can determine future progress.

This manual can be used in a variety of ways. Music educators on the college level may use this manual as a teaching tool, a guide for student teachers (Appendix A contains a tested outline of extended field experiences for student and beginning teachers), and/or as a guide for field experiences throughout the four or five-year music education degree program. Seasoned professionals may want to use some of the field experiences to strengthen areas in which they feel weak. Less experienced teachers may find all of the experiences useful.

chapter 1

School values and the music educator

A series of orientation exercises which introduce the new teacher to the school as a whole. Field experiences include:

1. *Orientation*
2. *School Organization*
3. *School Services*
4. *Guidance*
5. *Goals*
6. *Evaluation*

The emphasis throughout this field experience manual will be upon a positive approach. Most teachers, when asked, say that they would like to have their rehearsals characterized by basically positive student-teacher and student-student interactions. There are a few within the music profession, however, who sincerely believe that competent musical performance must come at the expense of positive interactions. While there are some teachers within the music profession who are almost entirely disapproving and whose organizations do perform very well musically, this does not necessarily indicate that the teacher must have negative interactions for a high level of musical performance or high level of music learning to take place. Indeed, research in music education as well as in other areas of instruction has indicated repeatedly that effective learning can take place as easily with a "happy" atmosphere as within one characterized by a great deal of disapproval.

It would appear that music educators should strive to understand the issues and variables that operate within the music learning situation. There seem to be at least three very important classifications of potential reinforcement for the music student. One of these, and perhaps the most important, is the music itself. Many people enter the music profession and stay in it because of the personal pleasure that is afforded them through the performance, knowledge, listening, or composition of music. As parallel research in other areas indicates, since music itself is highly reinforcing, people can be motivated to go through some misery to be able to participate in the music experience. Have you known situations where this seemed to be the case?

Another variable evident in most organizations involves peer reinforcement. It is possible that the peer involvement and the *esprit de corps* established by many groups account for their high student popularity (i.e., reinforcing characteristics), thus explaining why some students find a band, orchestra, or chorus attractive and yet are not tremendously involved in the music. Also, it would appear that many musical organizations have a great deal of peer and social approval operating within their structures. These characteristics perhaps explain, at least to some degree, their high level of success.

The third consideration explaining why students might like the music situation is the *teacher*. The power of a teacher, whether a teacher of music or engaged in any other aspect of academic endeavor, has been substantiated throughout research to be extremely consequential (i.e., reinforcing). The model music educator is generally not only a good musician and group leader but is a fine human being as well.

Nevertheless, the above three variables need to be separately analyzed, at least to some degree, in any attempt to explain why students would find a music experience desirable. It could well be that many students put up with an extremely disapproving conductor because they find the music and/or the social aspects of the group to be tremendously reinforcing. Therefore, it is possible for a conductor who is very disapproving actually to believe that students are responding to his/her teaching, when in fact students may be responding to the music or to the social aspects accompanying the performing experience.

It would probably be instructive for you to contemplate for a moment about your past participation within musical organizations to determine more precisely what contingencies accounted for your remaining in, and choosing, music as a career. Sometimes the contingencies change. As a student matures, different aspects of the musical, social, and interpersonal experience become more important. The music student may respond differentially to musical situations depending on age, friends, or school. Stop for a moment and ask yourself what circumstances operated in your life from your first start in the field of music through your entire musical career to the present. Try to weigh the above aspects as far as your own musical development was concerned. Why did you stay in the music group? Why did you not quit when others quit? Was it possible that you received a great deal of encouragement, or perhaps disapproval, from circumstances or persons outside of the school environment? Did it please your parents for you to perform? Did it please your parents that you were involved in a music activity? Did it ever *displease* anyone that you were in music? What *were* the contingencies operating in your past?

As previously stated, while this particular observation and field experience manual stresses a positive approach, this positive approach is not to be viewed as a cure-all for all teaching problems. The rationale for a positive approach lies in what most teachers say they believe about interaction patterns within their own teaching situations. It has been determined that most teachers, while saying that they want to be primarily positive, actually behave in classrooms in mostly disapproving ways. Previous research has indicated that very few teachers, kindergarten through high school, actually dispense more approval for appropriate social behavior than give disapproval for inappropriate behavior.[1] Thus, we have a discrepancy between the stated values of most teachers and what actually goes on within the classroom environment. Studies done in music situations indicate that there is often even more disapproval within some music organizations than there is within other academic situations. However, recent research indicates that basically *positive* approaches within choruses, bands, and orchestras, as well as in general and elementary music classes, are effective in fostering a high degree of musical competence. A music teacher can be highly approving and accomplish as much, if not more, in increasing student musical competencies and enhancing positive interpersonal interactions. Furthermore, it is conjectured that one of the reasons some music personalities have been able to evidence such a high degree of disapproval is precisely because of the other positive contingencies that operate within a musical performing organization. Perhaps if these same conductors were teaching less preferred subject matter, it would become necessary for them to develop more approving techniques in order to retain the interest and enthusiasm of their constituents. It should also be remembered that professionals are paid to perform.

A POSITIVE APPROACH

As long as recorded history and very probably long before, there have been teachers—teachers and students. Most students profess interest in learning and most teachers in teaching, yet often little teaching goes on and perhaps even less learning. Some pupils begin complaining about teachers and teaching practices before they begin to seriously evaluate any other aspect of their lives. From the lower grades through graduate school one hears constant rumblings concerning educational practices which at best are deemed irrelevant, at worst spitefully vindictive. Only occasionally are reports of excellence voiced. The thoughtful person may look past apparent idiosyncrasies and trivia to ask some basic questions: Why is this educational situation extant? What happens in the teacher-learning process to elicit unhappy responses? Are most teachers committed to misery for themselves as well as their students? Do people enter the teaching profession to promote ineffectual learning?[2]

In answer to the above questions, the authors think not; neither do we believe that educational processes are so complex as to defy analysis and subsequent improvement. It appears true but unfortunate that several important changes occur with many music teachers in that extremely short transition period from naive idealist to competent practitioner. The desire to be a good teacher often gives way first to disillusionment, then to cynicism, and perhaps on to despair. The culmination of this process is often complete resignation and apathy.

Perhaps the most difficult aspect for student teachers is the realization that there is a tremendous gap between ideas and actual behavior. Most people who enter the music profession desire to be good teachers. Often, this desire is accompanied with positive thoughts surrounding a previous music teacher of tremendous personal importance. As students study other subjects as well as music, additional student-teacher encounters add to the prospective teacher's idea of what teaching is all about. However, many of these encounters are characterized by negative interactions. It is not uncommon, therefore, for the prospective music educator to find him- or herself in a situation characterized by several aspects: one, a desire to be a good teacher; two, a desire to emulate a highly revered model from the past; and three, a requirement to absorb many additional models that probably represent the antithesis of what the student teacher wants to emulate.

The basic problem is that none of these aspects seems to prepare the prospective teacher to actually interact in a positive way within the classroom or rehearsal situation. While desire to be a good teacher seems to be extremely beneficial and perhaps a prerequisite for entering the teaching profession, it is often found that this desire quickly dissipates when actually directing a musical group or in teaching elementary or general music classes. The problem is that desire to be a good teacher must be operationalized before and during the initial student teaching period. If a prospective teacher's *desire* is to become an effective teacher, then this desire must be made evident to the students. Sometimes this is not the case. Many teachers seem ill-prepared to interact with students, and upon entering a real teaching situation their desire to be a good teacher wanes as they find themselves in more and more negative student-teacher interactions. One of the most difficult aspects of becoming a good teacher is to learn how to elicit desired responses from students. While this involves musicianship and skilled conducting techniques, it also includes many other behaviors which must be systematically mastered if one is to become a good teacher.

Also, it is often likely that prospective teachers have had a memorable teacher in their own backgrounds from whom they might have learned many behaviors. As with desire, however, a tremendous dichotomy seems to exist between what a student remembers about how that teacher taught and what the model teacher of the past actually did. Many times after students have been to college for just a short period, they return home for vacation or holidays and are disheartened to find that their old band, chorus, or orchestra is not nearly as good now as it was when they were in the group just a few months previous. This common phenomenon is probably attributable to the greater level of sophistication attained by the music major in just those few short months. This situation is much the same as the emulation of a past teacher. Often the memorable teacher is viewed in the eyes of a child or at least a somewhat naive musician. Evaluation becomes even more difficult if the teacher was not a high school or junior high school teacher but a grade school teacher. In grade school there is an even greater discrepancy between what the teacher actually does and how students perceive the teacher. It is extremely difficult, therefore, for a prospective teacher, during student teaching, to emulate a past teacher. This difficulty becomes exacerbated if what the past teacher did is not consistent with the personal "style" of the student teacher. Even if some ideas have been acquired from former models, the discrepancy between ideas and behavior makes it extremely difficult to teach as one perceived those models.

As for the last aspect of preparation, the experience of many negative teaching models (many of whom were perhaps encountered within the college experience), there still exists the main problem for the student teacher—what to do? Regardless of how many negative models the student teacher might have had, and granting that things learned from these negative models represent extremely important information (i.e., what *not* to do), the student teacher is still left in a quandary concerning how to behave. Thus, it becomes apparent that the desire to be a good teacher, having a previous excellent model, as well as many negative models, does not necessarily prepare the prospective teacher with much positive technique that can be utilized in the development of musical and educational competencies. *The prospective teacher must develop skills.* These skills should be behaviorally evident and should be practiced continuously if the teacher expects to gain the most benefit from the teaching experience.

Activities provided in this observation and field manual are specifically intended to develop competencies for the student and beginning teacher and to ensure that ideas are indeed translated into behaviors. Scientific investigation of many of these activities within carefully done studies has demonstrated the many changes possible when music teachers systematically apply behavioral principles in teacher-student interaction patterns. Research has indicated that most teachers do not fully realize how they are interacting with students. But when teachers interact in a purposeful way with feedback provided from objective recording techniques, they are indeed able to translate their ideas into behaviors and thereby gain the kind of musical and academic learning they desire.

The teacher is probably the most powerful and perhaps the most important source of productive rehearsal behavior. Teachers have been able to induce happier classroom environments, increase classroom efficiency, and enhance musical learning and aesthetic experience. Behavioral principles have been applied across many different situations to help the teacher develop specific teaching skills.

While all teachers are in fact modifying behavior within the music situation, the behavioral observer is able to observe systematically the classroom or rehearsal and demonstrate how and when the teacher is or is not effective. While some teachers, through trial and error, develop competencies for more effective learning in the rehearsal or general music situation, often this increase comes at a high price in frustration and negative control. Sometimes results appear to be even "magical" as opposed to concrete to the very teachers who are themselves engaged in the process. The cliché—"That conductor knows what she/he wants and knows how to get it"—appears to be the closest that many prospective teachers get to truly understanding, let alone developing, the competencies that are necessary for effective music teaching.

MODES OF FEEDBACK

Ongoing assessment of actual classroom and rehearsal behavior within music education is important in providing accurate feedback to the teacher. There appear to be two very distinct ways in which the teacher may be given feedback. The more traditional way is to have an evaluator observe the teacher throughout a rehearsal or class lesson. After the rehearsal is over, the evaluator tells the teacher what was done correctly and/or what could have been done differently in order to achieve more effective musical results. While this traditional form of feedback is extremely beneficial, it typically represents how the evaluator would have taught. This feedback often does not concern what the teacher actually *did,* but rather what the evaluator would have done had he/she been the teacher. Nevertheless, this traditional mode of feedback represents important information for the teacher.

A second, and entirely different observational system, is the system presented within this manual. The basic strategy underlying the following observational experiences does not involve what the evaluator would do but concentrates on recording in detail what the teacher is doing. These observational results are then given to the teacher to better decide whether or not his/her actual behavior represents his/her intent. It has been the experience of the authors that when teachers are given this kind of factually precise feedback, they will change their teaching behavior to come more in line with what they actually want to achieve within the classroom or rehearsal situation. Thus, with the help of the feedback provided by the observer/evaluator (or via videotape, audiotape, and other means of self-observation), the teacher comes to realize not only how ideas are translated into behavior but also the relationship of actual rehearsal and classroom *techniques,* to the teacher's *goals.* These observations provide necessary information so that teachers can change whatever they desire in order to become more effective music educators.

It is this approach to evaluation that necessitates the keeping of precise records throughout the entire teaching experience. The time log which you will be asked to keep will become extremely useful in analyzing and restructuring your professional time. Additionally, records of students' social and music behavior as well as teacher behavior will provide the specific information that you will need as you progress through your professional teaching experience. It is important to realize that it is your responsibility to develop the philosophies, behaviors, and techniques that you believe to be important within the rehearsal or classroom environment.

WHAT THE TEACHER DOES IS WHAT THE STUDENTS GET

The basic premise upon which each of these recording instruments is based is that the values and goals of a teacher are more related to what the teacher does than what he or she might believe they are doing. This is much like assessing people's musical values on the basis of how they spend their time, efforts, and money for music, not on what they might say about music. For example, if one were to ask you for a representative sample of your music taste, would this musical taste be represented through your record collection? Through your music library? Would it be the same as your choice of radio stations or other media? Would it be the same if one observed your concert attendance? Regardless of the disparities that might exist between what one says and what one does, research indicates that in classroom situations it is indeed what the teacher does that is translated into ideas and behaviors on the student's part. It does not appear to be too important that a teacher desires to have a positive rehearsal atmosphere if rehearsal comments are over 80% disapproving. From a musical point of view, it does not matter if the conductor or classroom teacher just thinks about working on phrasing or intonation if the teacher actually never works on phrasing or intonation. Students do not always respond to what teachers do, but it is extremely difficult for students to be responsive to ideas within the teacher's head that are never translated into demonstrable behaviors. These "behaviors" may be just a tiny nod or taking a breath, or making an extremely subtle conducting gesture, but they must be evident to the student. It is precisely for this reason that the subsequent parts of this manual are provided. As teachers develop more refined techniques for data collecting and analysis, they will be able to structure more effective techniques to more closely approximate musical desires or value systems.

The final and perhaps most important aspect of teaching concerns honest assessment of contingencies that operate in reinforcing the music teacher. If you are going to spend your life in music education, it appears quite important to understand precisely what behaviors are actually subsumed within that career. Most student teachers enter the teaching profession because of an "idea" concerning teaching music but without much awareness of the other behaviors necessary to become successful music educators. The idea of a fine performing group, the idea of a well-received concert, the idea of an innovative marching band, the idea of children responding enthusiastically to the elements of music are not necessarily the same as the corresponding behaviors that may or may not include these particular aspects within music learning.

It would seem that if a teacher is not personally reinforced by the rehearsal, by the musical process, by ongoing involvement in gradually shaping greater musical awareness, then the reinforcement that comes from an occasional concert would not have the necessary magnitude to sustain day-to-day teaching. It is extremely easy to dream of a fine performing group or to become involved with the idea of stimulating children's creativity toward greater aesthetic awareness. It is easy to become emotionally involved in the magic of music and somehow hope that this magic is constant and that the level of personal reinforcement afforded the teacher will be continuously high. However, it is easily observed, especially by those teachers who have been teachers for some time, that this is not necessarily the case. Student teachers need to develop not only long-range goals in order to receive the enjoyment that comes from the attainment of those goals, but also to develop the personal satisfaction that a teacher should receive when someone finally remembers to push down second valve for f-sharp, or not take a breath in the middle of the phrase, or to be happy when a youngster finally remembers to put the bells away, or that glorious feeling when someone is attentive, excited, and perhaps, even, in tune. It is assumed that a teacher's long-term reinforcement will most certainly come from the accumulation of positive techniques that are developed in the day-to-day process of introducing students to our expanding world of music.

FIELD EXPERIENCES

1. Orientation

Whether student teaching, beginning your first year of teaching, or having moved to a new school, your first concern should be getting acquainted with the school as a whole: administration, staff, faculty, students, physical plant, and daily routine. Since first impressions are often important in establishing rapport, you should immediately try to establish a positive and happy interaction with every individual you meet. To ensure that you are giving a positive impression, remember to smile as much as you can, be positive and enthusiastic when speaking, use eye contact, and be a careful listener rather than a rambling, off-task talker. Allow others to help you adjust to the new situation and be overtly appreciative of their help.

After meeting all the people who will most directly affect your professional life (principal, assistant principal, secretaries, guidance counselors, librarians, custodians, nearby faculty members, students in your classes), take some time to thoroughly explore the physical plant. Obviously, you will have found your own classroom and the school's main offices by this time. Other important places you should locate might include rest rooms, cafeteria, library, audio-visual storage area, nurse's office, guidance office, and custodian's office.

Finally, you should learn the school's daily schedule, conduct code, and fire-drill procedures. The faculty handbook will be a very valuable resource for this information. It should be read thoroughly *before* the first day since you will be held responsible for all information it contains.

In summary, the first two or three days of each student teaching or teaching experience will be a period of orientation. During this period you should do the following:

a. Set up an atmosphere of positive and happy interaction between you and your colleagues. Try to make all of your statements positive and enthusiastic. Listen carefully.

b. Find (1) the music classroom in which you will be teaching (or your home base if there is not a music classroom) (2) the school's main offices (3) rest room (4) the library (5) the audio-visual storage room (6) the cafeteria (7) the guidance counselor's office (8) the nurse's office (9) the custodian's office.

c. Learn the school's daily schedule.

d. Meet the principal, the secretary, other music teachers, teachers in neighboring classrooms, and the custodian.

e. Learn your daily class routine.

f. Learn students' names as quickly as possible, especially those be-having *appropriately*. These are the ones you'll want to reinforce.

g. Learn the fire-drill procedures.

Although you will be primarily concerned with survival in the classroom during the first week of teaching, you should schedule at least one hour a day to investigate various aspects of the school system, school organization, and school services. Knowledge of these is important for the development of your music program. The following are suggested questions which you will want to explore systematically through inter-views or school publications. Remember to keep a record for future reference.

2. School Organization

a. Is there a school board? How many members are on the board? If they are elected, how often and for what terms? Learn the names and occupations of the school board members. List their chief duties on the school board. What is their governing relationship to the system?

b. What is the superintendent's name? Is the person elected or ap-pointed? A professional educator or educational layperson?

c. How many assistant superintendents are there? What are their titles and designated responsibilities?

d. At least one system has the following staff organization. Try to draw an organizational chart for the system in which you teach.

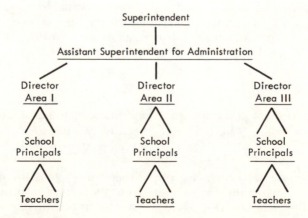

e. What networks are set up for systemwide communications between elementary, junior high or middle school, senior high school princi-pals and teachers?

f. Who is responsible for recruiting, interviewing, and hiring music teachers in your system? Who evaluates, recommends assignments, and recommends termination of employment for music teachers in your system? How is the music staff organized? Is there a music supervisor? What are the responsibilities of the supervisor?

g. Is there a teacher's union? NEA? How does it function? Does it negotiate directly with the Board of Education?

3. School Services

a. School Library

(1) What kinds of music reference materials are available? Periodicals? Biographies?

(2) Are recordings available? What kinds? Is there a listening staton? Can records be checked out?

b. Health Program

(1) Is there a school nurse?

(2) What does a teacher do if a student gets hurt or becomes ill?

c. Audio-visual and other technical media—instructional aids.

(1) What equipment is available in your school? Television? Slide projector? Film projector? Tape recorder? Overhead or opaque projector?

(2) Where do you get supplies such as audiotape, videotape, grease pencils, etc.?

(3) What kinds of audio-visual equipment (available in your school) could you use to set up independent learning stations? Describe or design three independent learning stations indicating how they would be used by students.

4. Guidance

Arrange to meet and interview the guidance counselor in the school in which you teach. The following checklist of questions will help you understand the role of guidance in regard to your teaching.

a. How does the performance group director in a school identify eligible students moving into his school from another (i.e., junior high to senior high school)? Does the system administer musical aptitude or achievement tests?

b. How does the guidance counselor identify students with special problems—low achievers, potential dropouts, personality problems, delinquents, etc.? How does the guidance counselor define the role of the music teacher when working together in these areas? How does the guidance counselor define the limits of the music teacher in advising students about personal problems?

c. How does the guidance counselor evaluate the effectiveness of the guidance program? How adequate are records on individual students? What provisions are made for records to be readily available to teachers? Do teachers use background information on their students?

d. How are grades assigned or what kind of reporting and evaluation is made in the area which you teach? Are tests valid, reliable, and is there any attempt at item analysis? What are the criterion behaviors which are measured? Does the student understand what behavior achieves high and low grades? What is the effect of grading on the student?

5. Goals

a. Does the music staff seem to understand the general educational philosophy and practices of the school system?

b. Are music teachers working in an area for which they are well prepared by education and experience?

c. Throughout the music program are there agreed-to goals and objectives and are members of the faculty working in terms of these?

d. Do any parts of the program seem to overshadow other parts? Are parts of the program neglected?

e. Are music teachers' teaching loads generally equal to loads in other teaching areas?

f. Does the school sponsor in-service training opportunities for professional leave—attendance at workshops and professional conferences?

g. Are the services of music specialists available to elementary classroom teachers? Do music specialists have a good working relationship with elementary classroom teachers?

6. Evaluation

a. Precisely what accountability is provided for music instruction at all levels of the program?

b. How are measurements, or grades, given in music? Are tests based on measurement of class objectives? Are any achievement tests given in music?

c. Examine the reports which are made to parents at the elementary, junior high or middle school, and senior high school levels. What kind of information about the student in *nonmusic courses* is provided for parents? In *music* courses?

The purpose of this field experience outline is to acquaint student teachers and first-year teachers with prevailing school/community values. It is especially important that student teachers practice this technique of investigating school values for future use. An understanding and empathy for the problems encountered by people who will be significant to the development of a music program is of utmost importance for attaining long-term musical goals.

If, as a result of your investigation of the school's organization, services, guidance, goals, and evaluation, you find that the values of the school system are quite a bit different from your own values as a teacher, you may feel uncomfortable remaining within that school system. On the other hand, by having the knowledge of these values, you may be able to shape your own values and create a more effective and stimulating school music program for your students.

NOTES

[1]Clifford K. Madsen and Jayne M. Alley, "The Effect of Reinforcement on Attentiveness: A Comparison of Behaviorally Trained Music Therapists and Other Professionals with Implications for Competency Based Academic Preparation," *Journal of Music Therapy,* 16 (Summer 1979), pp. 70–82.

[2]Charles H. Madsen, Jr., Clifford K. Madsen, and Don F. Driggs, "Freeing Teachers to Teach," in *Behavioral Intervention in Human Problems,* ed. H. C. Rickard (New York: Pergamon Press, 1971), p. 61.

chapter 2

Developing resource materials

Techniques for the development of a comprehensive resource file through systematic analysis of books, periodicals, recordings, musical scores, other materials, and structured conversations with experienced professionals. Field experiences include:

1. *Developing a Resource File*
2. *Structuring Conversations with Experienced Music Teachers*

A time-worn saying in music education runs: "That conductor knows what she/he wants and knows how to get it." Generally this cliché refers to a specific music situation where a conductor is rehearsing a particular organization. However, the cliché can be analyzed in a much broader sense than that which would only apply to one specific musical group or one performing situation. The first part of it refers to a conductor or music educator knowing what she/he desires in the way of specific musical competencies. Yet, the phrase, "That conductor knows what he/she wants . . ." presupposes many other things as well. Most often it also implies that the conductor is an excellent musician who not only understands the musical score but also has the ability to place that particular piece of music within a broader musical perspective. There are those who would say that it should also indicate that the conductor is primarily concerned with eliciting an excellent performance. Others might add that this excellence should be subsumed within an aesthetic awareness regarding both the performers and the listeners.

There seem to be many musicians who accept the first part of the cliché entirely. Their view of conducting assumes that if the conductor is an excellent musician and has been well prepared in the art of conducting, then positive musical results will be forthcoming. If this represents the entire case, then most of the time spent in the preparation of such a person would involve activities directed toward knowledge, understanding, performance, and application of the musical art. This is certainly to be desired and perhaps is the most important aspect of preparation in effective music education. However, the concept should go even further. Ideally, a person who completes a degree in music education should have the ability, even without a music library or any facilities, to compose, organize, and present a complete musical experience for all students in grades K-12. While this may seem completely unrealistic and overly ambitious, it would still embody the best of musical preparation. Musicians so prepared could certainly be extremely independent in structuring musical activities.

This type of preparation, or anything even remotely resembling it, does not seem to be the case. Indeed, the present state of music education seems to include some graduates who are so insecure of their ability to select musical experiences and interpret the music selected that they are in constant search of anyone who might show them "what music to select and how the music goes." It is not uncommon to find choral and instrumental directors, complete with scores and tape recorders, assiduously taping performances of particular music renditions in order to feel more comfortable in their own selection and interpretation. When a music educator is secure in his or her selection of music experiences for the ensemble or the general music group, then recording of another interpretation or seeking out a different viewpoint is to be commended. The analysis of another musician's interpretation would then provide yet another avenue of help to the music teacher in preparing the piece. If, however, this dedication to finding out "how the piece is played" constitutes the *only* interpretation or is intended primarily to absolve the director of the responsibility to be musically independent, then certainly it is to be avoided. One would hope that every music educator would have enough experience and knowledge to be able to choose literature appropriate to a particular organization and also feel comfortable in analyzing and interpreting the music appropriately. Thus, the first part of the cliché, "That conductor knows what she/he wants," could conceivably be interpreted to include musical independence that, although rare, should be sought by every musician.

The second part of the cliché ("and knows how to get it") implies specific techniques used to realize an intended musical effect. The effect might have to do with preparing a specific musical performance, or it may concern other aspects of music making, or music activities for younger children. Regardless, it would seem that every music educator should know what they want and have some procedures for getting that particular effect from performers/students. Often, a teacher may have a very good idea of what she/he wants yet not be capable of eliciting that precise musical effect from a group of students. The music educator must be careful, however, not to assume that the procedures and processes involved in achieving desired musical responses represent only "gimmicks" and "tricks" that can be collected over a period of time from outstanding clinicians and teaching models. It seems unfortunate that there are many inexperienced music educators who believe that the best, if not the only, way to develop the art of effective rehearsal techniques is to amass isolated procedures or "good ideas" that have been garnered over the years from seemingly effective teachers. The inexperienced music educator should be diligent in exploring effective techniques, guidelines, and sets of principles that can be used for effective instruction and not limit information to those individual bits of knowledge that fall under the heading "this worked for me."

A competency-based approach to music education suggests that there are certain cognitive, affective, and psychomotor skills that can be studied, systematically analyzed, and operationally defined toward effective instruction. There are many systematic approaches to teaching and learning that when put into a larger context can be very useful in helping any music educator get desired results from a music organization. However, to assume that a potpourri of activities, tips, and general testimonial statements constitutes the only useful body of information available is to ignore effective approaches that have been developed through careful systematic research in instruction.

It is understandable that some inexperienced music educators believe that effective techniques of music education constitute "one-hundred-and-one things that make music work for me." Even some articles and well-intended texts do not contain systematically developed and thoroughly organized procedures to be used in developing musical competencies. Also, it becomes apparent when observing certain music directors, that they do not represent the best models for effective instruction. When observing some conductors and classroom music teachers, it is often difficult to ascertain precisely what their overall goal or objective actually is. Such phrases as "You're flat, clarinets," "Watch me, altos," "Good phrasing, trombones," "I'll clap a rhythm and then you repeat it," may or may not represent effective interaction patterns toward a desired goal. Often, when one asks a director what he or she is doing (after observing such interactions at whatever level of instruction) the terminal objective becomes vague and obscure as the director rationalizes from an implied goal of excellent performance toward a vague concept of "aesthetic sensitivity." If a music educator's overall goal is to develop aesthetic responsiveness to aural stimuli, and if the director has specific objectives and strategies to implement that philosophy through sensitive performance, then goals and objectives appear both realistic and nested within a program that can be justified. However, this is often not the case. Vague allusions to aesthetic awareness are made only after the fact in order to justify whatever the conductor believes he or she is doing.

If aesthetic sensitivity or any other general goal can be operationally defined into specific observable behaviors, then these behaviors might be learned and in some way measured such that the goal of aesthetic education is not only realized but documented. An educator should be able to specify what he or she is doing in any teaching interaction in order to justify these experiences in some way other than by pretending that they exist by question-begging definition: "If you were truly sensitive you would understand," or "It's far too complicated and complex to be analyzed and specified systematically." Instead, that director might state, for example, that perfecting intonation within a clarinet section will lead to a more pleasing sound, which may also constitute a better performance, which also meets the objective of providing experiences that help develop aesthetic awareness. Unfortunately, there are some people who believe that the only way that one can have an aesthetic experience is to be unable to describe it.

One major rationale of a competency-based approach is that values which are specified by the teacher must be operationalized and systematically taught and learned so that clear goals are realized. A competency-based approach suggests that aesthetic awareness can indeed be developed through the systematic analysis and subsequent application of "knowing what one wants and knowing how to get it."

To the student teacher who is not sophisticated in analyzing the complex interaction patterns that can be observed in any music organization, it appears as though the process is *magic*. It may even seem that there is a certain magic in the music that somehow passes from the score through the conductor to the musicians and then to any listeners who may be present. Sometimes it is assumed that this magic can indeed be present because everyone desires it so much. It only takes a little observing, however, to determine that this is not the case. If there is magic in music (and most of us believe there is), it must be remembered that the magic does not lend itself to "magical processes" that are nonspecified and rely solely upon the pretense of extreme personal sensitivity. While it may appear that the process of music is "magical," it most certainly is not. Knowing what one wants and how to get it represents a lifelong pursuit of the art and science of music making. All aspects must be carefully analyzed, checked, and rechecked toward the goal of more efficient teaching and learning.

DEVELOPING INDEPENDENCE IN MUSIC SELECTION

One important aspect of a competency-based approach to music education is the gathering of materials and information for effective teaching. As has been previously stated, this should not represent an effort that begins only after graduation. Experienced teachers are continuously seeking new information. Yet it is impossible to know even how to get started without an early grounding in materials-gathering techniques necessary to be independent in subsequent music selection. Most often student and beginning music teachers will find themselves in a situation where a great deal of music materials are already present. For example, choral directors will generally find a choral library that, although perhaps dated, has some pieces that can be performed. Similarly, instrumental directors will usually find libraries containing some suitable material. In the general and elementary music areas, most often teachers will find that their schools have at least one basal series that has previously been used. Although certain books from the series might be missing, it can still be used in the instruction of students. Regardless of existing materials, the effective music educator needs to develop personal techniques and skills for selecting materials. This includes building one's personal library and references in order to effect goals and objectives consistent with a high level of music instruction.

There are many stories in music education circles about recent graduates who try to perform with their young and inexperienced students those same music selections that their directors performed while still in college. This is not only unfortunate, but also a tremendous disservice to those students who are asked to attempt difficult musical material with which they are not only unfamiliar but also which they are not capable of adequately performing. Alternately, there appear to be many resourceful undergraduates who are continuously attempting to find new sources and materials for potential use throughout their undergraduate training. Of course, this is to be commended. It cannot be stressed too much that the process for developing skills necessary for effective selection throughout one's musical career should start as early as possible. Sometimes specific courses are given toward this end. However, most often every musician must develop these techniques individually.

After appropriate materials have been chosen, then it is possible for the music educator to design musical learning activities appropriate for each specific situation. As was noted in Chapter One, it takes more than desire, trying to emulate an influential teacher, and avoiding bad models to be an effective music educator. The difficult aspects of being a music teacher come in the day-to-day activities and the continuous interaction patterns with students over time.

Ideals and values must be translated into actions. Even though many teachers believe in positive ideas, it would be difficult for many to specify observable behaviors in which students should engage. Most teachers believe students ought to be sensitive musicians, cooperative in rehearsal and group activities, and communicate effectively with each other and the teacher. Yet, for these ideas to be effectively taught they must be described with specificity such that competencies can be developed. The music educator must define values (ideas) so that a student can engage in some activity that promotes and operationalizes those ideas. Some evidence as to whether the student is developing these particular patterns of responses is also necessary. It is the specificity concerning overt behavioral responses and the measurement of these responses that constitutes a competency-based approach to music education. Ideas are generally made more specific as behaviors are observed and measured.

Obviously, the first step in structuring any music learning sequence is to define values so that the behavior of the student provides some indication that learning is actually taking place. In this regard specificity is the key to a competency-based approach. The teacher must be specific in determining precisely what the students will do in order to attain the necessary and desired competencies. Evaluation of competencies provides the information necessary for the teacher to be sure that students are learning what the teacher expects. Formal and informal tests provide some indication of academic and musical competencies. Other indices of measurement must be developed for the more difficult concepts embodied within aesthetic awareness. It is possible, however, for the music teacher to learn to assess as well as develop specific activities and responses that contribute to aesthetic growth. Even feelings can be objectively measured so that the teacher receives some indication that the student does indeed understand.

Music teachers have been providing experiences for students of all ages for years. Often a competency-based approach represents nothing more than objectively classifying these experiences in a systematic manner and organizing teaching activities so that there is more of a relationship among the activities. Students are thereby provided with the transferable skills that contribute to a holistic approach. Teachers are continuously getting feedback from students concerning their activities, and many times decisions are made that enhance the music experience. However, some decisions that ought to be made on a sound curricular basis are sometimes made in relationship to how attentive, how involved, or how active students become while engaging in certain music experiences. While it is important to ascertain student enthusiasm, the variables in analyzing teacher/student interactions should not be limited to a short-term assessment of students' likes or dislikes of particular music tasks or performing experiences. This should not be the sole criterion in the selection of particular activities or pieces to perform.

Ideally, a complete music program should proceed from the philosophy and values of the teacher, students, and community. Materials should be developed that coincide and implement the value systems of all concerned. Perhaps the most important aspect of selecting appropriate materials is first determining a philosophy of music teaching with which all feel comfortable. In addition to one's own philosophy of music teaching, it is essential to analyze the philosophies of the school system (music supervisor, principal, parents, teachers, and others) regarding music. Chapter One provides techniques for investigating these school and community values. Compromises may be necessary to insure musical happiness for a wide variety of people. Regardless of the difficulties involved in this process, more meaningful musical goals can be established if philosophical differences have been resolved. Too often, for *short-term* musical and teaching happiness, materials are chosen before philosophical issues have been dealt with because this is easier. However, these materials become "just used," resulting in little or no *long-term* musical learning and happiness. If existing available materials are "just used," then the learning derived from these experiences constitutes its own predetermined value. In this case the teacher does not get to decide because the materials used have already decided. Selecting materials is certainly one of the most important aspects of music education. The beginning teacher should take great care to develop this skill which plays a vital part in providing the student with increased independence.

FIELD EXPERIENCES

1. Developing a Resource File

Certainly one of the most important things you will accomplish throughout your career as a teacher is increasing your knowledge of methods and materials for elementary, middle school, junior high school, and senior high school music teaching. In general, the collection of these methods and materials will be guided both by your goals as a music teacher and by the curriculum approved by your school district. For example, the materials and methods collected by elementary music teachers will be quite different from those collected by secondary school music teachers. Furthermore, the collection of methods and materials by an elementary music teacher teaching in a school district using the Kodaly method exclusively will be quite different from that collected by a music teacher in a district which supports an eclectic approach to music teaching.

Therefore, in developing an ongoing file and/or log of methods and materials one may decide to (1) include all possible methods, materials, books, articles, technological media, and other resources; (2) select the best from all possible resources; or (3) select resources based on a specified curriculum. Prospective and beginning music teachers should probably select the first alternative. As one gains experience in teaching, the ability to critically analyze and select the best methods and materials is sharpened. Thus, with experience, the process of gathering knowledge becomes more efficient and takes less time.

In gathering materials for more effective teaching, the beginning music teacher should first look at the actual materials if at all possible, rather than relying solely on catalog information or selective lists. After this initial analytical and critical look at the materials, try to talk with an experienced music teacher who has used the materials about their effectiveness in the classroom or rehearsal. When you study particular aspects of teaching music (Orff, Kodaly, Suzuki, Manhattanville), try to go to the original source first rather than to adaptations. Workshops in these various music methodologies can be very helpful after you have prepared for them by studying the method. In selecting music for performance groups, review selected lists for festivals and contests, study reviews of music in periodicals, study scores thoroughly, listen to available recordings, and attend reading clinics. Always seek the opinion of experienced music teachers whenever possible.

In the development of your own resource file nothing substitutes for *your* personal ability to analyze, criticize, and select stimulating, challenging, and perhaps even entertaining materials and methods for your students. After a variety of meaningful inputs through the resources mentioned above, you should be able to make a final decision concerning what you can use most successfully in your own teaching situation. Here are some suggestions for developing your resource file:

a. Suggested Materials

(1) Several cardboard or metal 5 × 8 card files
(2) Blank 5 × 8 indexes, ⅓ cut
(3) Blank 5 × 8 cards
(4) Repertory card forms (see Appendices C and D)
(5) Typewriter (It is always advisable to type information you plan to keep for a long period of time.)

b. Card File Headings

(1) Books and Periodicals
　(a) Books concerning general music education, music theory and history, music literature and appreciation, general music encyclopedias, and so forth (see figure 2-1 for Book Card example)
　(b) Periodicals concerning all aspects of music, music education, and general education (see figure 2-2 for Periodical Card example).

```
Baker, Theodore. Baker's Biographical Dictionary of Musicians. 5th Ed.
    Revised by Nicolas Slonimsky. New York: G. Schirmer, 1958.

    By far the best biographical dictionary in English—long lists of
works—exact dates of 1st performances of works—musicologists listed plus
list of their books and/or articles

    performers and outstanding teachers also listed—tries to eliminate
many myths surrounding composers and their works

    publishers, librettists, and other people who have connection with
music are included

    no illustrations or cross-ref.
```

Figure 2-1 Book Card Example

```
Journal of Research in Music Education. Reston, Virginia: Music Educa-
    tors National Conference. Published Quarterly.

    Contains the latest historical, philosophical, descriptive, and experi-
mental research findings in music education. Each article is preceded by an
abstract. Reviews of recently published books are also included.

    Current editor is James C. Carlsen, University of Washington.
```

Figure 2-2 Periodical Card Example

(2) Music for Performance and Study: You may want to cross-reference
for various difficulty levels of the music. Some performance literature might be equally appropriate for an advanced middle school
and a rebuilding high school.

(a) Solos (see figures 2-3 and 2-4)

(b) Choral Music (see figure 2-5), possible subdivisions: unison, two-
part, SSA, TTB, SSAA, TTBB, SATB, Double Chorus, and
SATB divisi

(c) Instrumental Music (see figure 2-6), possible subdivisions: orchestra (full orchestra, strings only, elementary, middle school,
junior high school, senior high school); band (wind ensemble,
concert band, marching band, jazz ensemble, elementary middle
school, junior high school, and senior high school)

SOLO MUSIC ANALYSIS

Instrument/voice classification <u>Low Voice</u>

Title <u>Wie Melodien Zieht Es Mir, Op. 105, No. 1</u>

Composer/Arranger <u>Johannes Brahms</u>

Publisher <u>G. Schirmer – Fifty Selected Songs</u>

Catalog Number <u>Vol. 1755</u> (SELECTED) REJECTED

(DIFFICULT) MEDIUM EASY

Range and tessitura (range notated in white notes; tessitura in black notes)

Text (for vocal solos): in German

Dynamic Range: p – mf

Phrase Length: 4+ measures long

Rhythm: $\frac{4}{4}$ meter--2 pulses per measure--in voice part quarter note

        prolation--some dotted rhythms ♩. ♪

Accompaniment: arpeggiated eighth notes--thin rather than thick texture
        good for "small" voice

Technical Problems (embellishments, articulation, embouchure, special effects,
    range, tessitura, fingerings, bowing, intonation, etc.):
    Need good breath control for long phrases--intonation problems
    may occur in upper part of range

Other Comments: for very advanced high school soloist

Figure 2-3 Solo Music Analysis Example: Vocal

SOLO MUSIC ANALYSIS

Instrument/voice classification   <u>Trumpet in B♭ (lst Mvt.)</u>

Title   <u>Trumpet Concerto</u>

Composer/Arranger   <u>Johann Nepomuk Hummel   Ed. Armando Ghitalla</u>

Publisher   <u>Robert King Music Co.</u>

Catalog Number   <u>Music for Brass Number 801</u>   SELECTED   REJECTED

           <u>DIFFICULT</u>   MEDIUM   EASY

Range and tessitura (range notated in white notes; tessitura in black notes)

Text (for vocal solos):

Dynamic Range: p-f

Phrase Length: Basically 4 measures

Rhythm: Simple with some ornamentation

Accompaniment: Orchestral reduction for piano--tends to be difficult

Technical Problems (embellishments, articulation, embouchure, special effects,
    range, tessitura, fingerings, bowing, intonation, etc.):
    1. Endurance 2. Intervallic skip 12-13 after G presents control and
    intonation problems 3. Intonation at I (key of D♭) 4. Control of
    intervallic skips and trill pattern between O and P.

Other Comments:
        A standard work in the trumpet repertoire. Valuable in
        the study of Classical concerto style. Excellent historical
        notes included in the piano score.

Figure 2-4 Solo Music Analysis Example: Instrumental

CHORAL MUSIC ANALYSIS

Title Wondrous cool, thou woodland quiet (Op. 62, No. 3)

Composer/Arranger Johannes Brahms - edited by Franz Wasner

Voice Parts   SATB   Publisher G. Schirmer

Catalog Number   9335   (SELECTED)   REJECTED

DIFFICULT   (MEDIUM)   EASY

Appeal: Sophisticated high school chorus

Range and tessitura (range notated in white notes; tessitura in black notes)

Text: English text by Henry S. Drinker after the original by Paul
     Heyse--no German text

Dynamic Range: pp-f

Phrase Length: 2-3 measures

Melody: disjunct melody line--some awkward leaps and chromatic alterations--
     each voice is melodically important--bass line is difficult

Harmony: D major modulating to A major and back to D major with chromatic
     alterations throughout

Texture: basically homophonic--middle of each verse contains somewhat
     contrapuntal treatment (upper voices versus lower voices)

Rhythm: tricky cross rhythms in middle of each verse may result in
     missed or awkward entrances--may also cause loss of legato style

Form: Strophic--three verses

Accompaniment: Piano part (for rehearsal only)

Size of Chorus (Recommendation Only):30 or smaller--but nice musical
     experience for larger groups too

The Printed Page: very good

Other Comments: Need two or three basses who can sing low "f"
     comfortably--lower bass pitches can be optional

Figure 2-5 Choral Music Analysis Example

INSTRUMENTAL MUSIC ANALYSIS

Title Second Suite in F for Military Band (1st Mvt.)

Composer/Arranger Gustav Holst

Instrumentation Symphonic Band

Publishers Boosey & Hawkes

Catalog Number OMB-201   SELECTED   REJECTED

            DIFFICULT   MEDIUM   EASY

Appeal: The entire four movement suite is founded on old English country
        tunes of which the first movement (March) contains three:
        "Morris Dance," "Swansea Town," and "Claudy Banks". Contrasts in
        meter ($\frac{2}{4}$, $\frac{6}{8}$), style (detached/legato), and ensemble (solo, brass
        band, full band) contribute to the musicality of the movement.

Possible range and/or tessitura problems (range notated in white notes;
tessitura in black notes)

Dynamic Range: pp-ff

Phrase Length: 8 measures

Melody: generally scalewise,
        few skips

Harmony: Consonant - use of contrasting
         keys: F maj./ B♭ min.

Texture: contrasting- Bar. solo with
         light accom./ Full Band-rich sonority

Rhythm: simple - use of contrasting
        duple/triple meters

Form: ABA

Other Comments: Reference to Frederick Fennell's detailed analysis of this
                piece in the November 1977 issue of The Instrumentalist
                will be of invaluable assistance in the preparation of this work.

Figure 2-6 Instrumental Music Analysis Example

    (d) Small Ensemble Music (see figures 2-5 and 2-6 for format), possible subdivisions: choral and instrumental duets, trios, quartets, quintets, madrigal group, chamber choir, brass choir, percussion ensemble, woodwind choir, etc.

    (e) Methods Books, possible subdivisions: strings, woodwinds, brass, percussion, vocal

    (f) Sightreading Materials (vocal and instrumental)

(3) Elementary Music Resources

    (a) Materials (see figure 2-7), possible subdivisions: films, filmstrips, recordings, A-V equipment, special materials for handicapped children, basal series, songs, musical games, and so forth

    (b) Musical Instruments (see figure 2-8)

    (c) Cross-reference material in #1 and #2 by grade level

(4) Current Topics in Music and Music Education (see figure 2-9 for Topic Card Example)

    (a) Sources containing written abstracts: *Psychological Abstracts, Dissertation Abstracts, Journal of Research in Music Education,* and others

    (b) Sources containing articles for which you must write your own abstract: *Music Educators Journal, Instrumentalist, Choral Journal,* and others

    (c) Possible subdivisions of this file: acoustics, pitch, sightreading, rhythm, music as reinforcement, biofeedback, programmed learning, independent learning stations, behavioral techniques in music, instructional technology, and others.

The above organization of materials into four divisions may not be appropriate for every individual developing a resource file. For example, some music teachers may want a more comprehensive file for "Music for Performance Study." In that case, it might be advisable to have separate files for each of the following: solos, choral music, instrumental music, small ensemble music, methods books, and sightreading material. Others may consider combining two areas into one card file, e.g., "Books and Periodicals" and "Current Topics in Music and Music Education."

Regardless of the final decision concerning the overall organization of the resource file, emphasis should be placed on the completeness of information contained on each card. This information should include everything you have observed about the book, periodical, music, film, filmstrip, recording, game, song, and research articles so that future reference to the card can be an effective substitute for looking at the actual material. In addition to bibliographical information (title, author, publisher, and so forth) and a summary of what the material contains and its purpose (preface, introduction, table of contents), you should

ELEMENTARY MATERIALS ANALYSIS

Title Music Duration Kit

Author Robert Testa

Publisher Education Enterprises, Inc. Date 1977

Grade Level Primary grades through Price ?
Junior High School
Format (book, records, pamphlets, series) game with dice—teacher's

manual provided

Comments on art work, recordings, songs, supplementary material, etc.
All game symbol pieces are proportionately scaled in size from

the eighth note rest to the whole note rest. The easel accomodates

eight full measures of notation.

Comments on type of children these materials might appeal to (ethnic, regional, social, cultural, intellectual level) All—provides means to

create rhythm patterns, take rhythmic dictation, and/or develop

rhythmic imagery

How can materials be used with special education classes or handicapped
children? Can help these students learn the function of meter

signatures, note and rest values, and single and double bar lines

How much work with instruments is there?
Instruments could be used with the kit in a game situation

Other Comments Teacher's manual provides good suggestions for

using this kit

Figure 2-7 Elementary Materials Analysis Example

ELEMENTARY MUSICAL INSTRUMENT ANALYSIS

Instrument Soprano Recorder

Manufacturer Yamaha

Grade Level Third Grade and older   Price $1.50

Key C   Materials made of Plastic

Availability of Parts not applicable   Expense of Parts - - - - - -

Will the instrument stand abuse? Yes

Will it stay in tune? Yes

Possible playing problems for children Overblowing--Hard for smaller

children to cover double holes in foot and middle joints--

Problems in holding instrument, especially fingering D (fourth line)--

Also difficult using half thumb hole to produce 2nd 8va--Attacks

and releases are difficult for younger children

Storage problems None--plastic covers provided

Maintenance Clean with soapy water instead of alcohol

Method books or music currently available? Chapter 3. Fundamental Classroom

Music Skills by Wachhaus and Kuhn

Overall reaction Like tone quality and intonation of this instrument

Figure 2-8 Elementary Musical Instrument Analysis Example

Topic: *Absolute Pitch*

Cuddy, Lola L. "Practice effects in the absolute judgment of pitch." *Journal of the Acoustical Society of America.* Vol. 43, No. 5. 1968.

The relationship between practice and absolute pitch recognition was studied. Experiment I indicated that subjects with musical training were more accurate in identifying pitches than subjects without musical training. Experiments II and III studied the relative merits of two methods of pitch recognition training. It was found that subjects who were systematically trained to A-440 recognized a series of ten pitches more accurately than subjects who received regular feedback on various pitches. The author concludes that training on a reference standard is more effective than regular feedback in developing absolute pitch.

Figure 2-9 Topic Card Example

make notes on how you might use the material in your classroom. Furthermore, you may also want to include opinions of other experienced teachers about the material.

2. Structuring Conversations with Experienced Music Teachers

One of the most efficient ways for beginning teachers to improve their music program professionally is to consult regularly with colleagues. One structured conversation per week with an experienced colleague can be most helpful and stimulating. The structured conversation is, in effect, a planned interview. A record should be kept of these conversations in the form of notes, cassette tapes, or reel-to-reel tapes. Topics can be selected from the following lists:

a. Secondary Schools

(1) Recruitment of students
(2) Budget/fund raising
(3) Uniforms: selecting, making, financing, maintaining
(4) Publicity: purposes, sources
(5) Awards: types, criteria, presentation
(6) Selection of music
(7) Concerts: how to organize, how to select a program for interest and teaching purposes
(8) Special problems of junior high students: changing voice, etc.

(9) Problems of teaching music in the junior high or middle school for the general student—Who teaches the course—Objectives—Attitudes of music teachers, students, teachers from other subject matter areas, and principal toward this course—Special problems of teaching music to the general student at this level

(10) Private music study

(11) Requisitioning and ordering procedures

(12) Lists of equipment and inventories

(13) Instrument rental and loans

(14) Equipment insurance

(15) Storage, handling, and care of equipment

(16) Filing, ordering, and managing music

(17) Use of audio-visual materials

(18) Boosters and parents organizations

(19) Student handbooks

(20) Rehearsal techniques and planning

(21) Scheduling

(22) Discounts on instruments—how to get a good price—used instruments—undersized instruments

(23) Performance groups: auditioned or nonauditioned

(24) Full score vs. condensed score

(25) Contests, festivals, competition: All-State, All-County

(26) Score reading and interpretation

(27) How to establish rapport with students

(28) Transporting students: parents' permission, insurance, teacher liability

b. Elementary School

(1) Time allotted to music instruction in the different grades: minutes per week or month

(2) Music teaching by the music teacher vs. music teaching by the classroom teacher

(3) Involving the classroom teacher in teaching music

(4) Music instruction for the classroom teacher through in-service training, workshops, etc.

(5) Elementary music as preparation for future participation of elementary students in chorus, band, and orchesta on the secondary level

(6) Specific problems encountered with each grade, K-6—physical, emotional, intellectual, disciplinary: their effect on teaching methods and choice of materials, specific techniques used to handle these problems

(7) Relating the arts on the elementary level

(8) Relating music to other academic subjects on the elementary level
(9) Materials: how to choose them and where to get them
(10) Budget/fund raising
(11) Performing groups
(12) Parents and booster clubs
(13) Publicity
(14) Equipment, insurance, and inventory
(15) Use of audio-visual materials

When you have selected a topic for your structured conversation, immediately refer to your card file. Successful interviews or structured conversations are those which have been prepared in advance. Therefore you will want to do as much research on the topic as possible before you contact an experienced colleague.

For example, suppose you have selected "recruitment" as a topic for a structured conversation. One of the first places you would want to look for information concerning recruitment would be the card file containing information on books and periodicals. Cards in this card file will direct you to various general music education books as well as to periodicals containing articles on recruitment such as the *Music Educators Journal.* When you go to these books and articles, you will find many suggestions for recruitment of students. Some of these suggestions might be to (1) provide current members of performing groups with reinforcing experiences (awards, uniform dress, recordings of performances) which can be observed by nonmembers who may then want to become involved so that they can receive these experiences themselves; (2) meet with the principal and/or guidance counselor to discuss schedule changes which might make membership in performance organizations more accessible; (3) obtain schedules of all students, listing those who have time for an additional course; (4) make personal contacts with students or have members of the group make personal contacts; (5) make posters; and (6) have a membership drive.

After you have done considerable research on the topic and made notes for yourself, make a list of questions which you will want to ask in your structured conversation. Considering the above information concerning recruitment, questions might include: (1) What kind of poster ideas have been most successful for you? (2) How did you get students involved in performance organizations? (3) If you are teaching in a secondary school, is it a good idea to make visits to elementary, middle schools, and junior high schools to begin recruitment early? If so, what kinds of things should you do on these visits? (4) How important are the guidance counselor and principal in getting new students interested in performance organizations? (5) How can you make personal contact with students without alienating them and without pleading with them to join? (6) What kinds of music and activities appeal to students in a school assembly? Is a school assembly a good recruitment device? (7) What technique do you use to put students at ease when you are auditioning them or talking to them?

As you see, the more research or planning that you do in advance of a structured conversation, the more questions you can generate, and thus the more information and answers you will have for future use.

Students in the public schools change from year to year. Therefore you cannot always depend solely upon books and articles from periodicals which quickly grow out of date for the latest techniques in teaching music. One of the best resources for good ideas and techniques are those experienced teachers who themselves have kept idea logs and have learned, sometimes through trial and error, what works and what does not work.

chapter 3

Developing a positive approach through observation

A systematic approach for the beginning teacher to examine specific student/teacher behaviors in both regular and music classrooms. Field experiences include:

1. *Learning Systematic Observation Techniques*
    a. *Preparing for Observation*
    b. *General Observation Procedures*
2. *Observation in the Regular Classroom*
    a. *Recording Student Behavior*
    b. *Recording Teacher Behavior*
3. *Using Observational Data to Improve Teaching and Learning in Music*
    a. *Observing Elementary Music Classes*
    b. *Observing Choral and Instrumental Rehearsals*
    c. *Observing Conductor Behavior*

It would seem that much learning can take place vicariously, that is, by observing someone else doing something which results in either positive or negative consequences. An observer can choose to act similarly if the behavior of the person observed has good results or he/she may choose to avoid that behavior if the reverse is true. Thus, vicarious learning, or *modeling*, is one of the most efficient ways to learn.

The work of Albert Bandura[1] provides extensive evidence concerning the effects of modeling on learning. He states that

> exposure to modeling influences has three clearly different effects. . . . First, an observer may acquire new response patterns that did not previously exist in his behavioral repertoire. . . . Second, observation of modeled actions and their consequences to the performer may strengthen or weaken inhibitory responses on observers. . . . Third, the behavior of others often serves merely as discriminative stimuli for the observer in facilitating the occurrence of previously learned responses in the same general class.[2]

In addition, Bandura emphasizes that an observer will fail to match the model's behavior if he/she does not attend to, recognize, or differentiate the distinctive features of the model's responses. Thus it is possible for a student to be in a fine performing organization with an excellent conductor and still not learn correct imitation responses regarding conducting.

The purpose of these field experiences in observation is to direct attention to what an effective teacher does which has proven to be effective (according to a vast amount of research data) in producing high levels of appropriate student behavior. In addition, these field experiences will focus on the systematic observation of specific, pinpointed, inappropriate (off-task) student behavior. Systematic observation helps one to direct attention to specified teacher and student behaviors, define categories of appropriate and inappropriate behavior, and differentiate the distinctive features of both teacher and student behavior. This is the first step for the beginning teacher toward acting in a more effective way in the music teaching situation.

One teaching technique to which attention will be directed is that of reinforcement. Reviews of behavioral research concerning approval/ disapproval teacher behavior[3] have indicated that praise generally acts as a facilitator to performance and is perhaps the easiest and most natural incentive for appropriate social behavior. Specifically, behavioral litera-ture to date indicates that (1) teacher attention in the form of praise, smiles, or reprimands, when made contingent upon the behaviors of students in a classroom, serves to increase the rate at which these be-haviors are repeated, regardless of the nature, positive or negative, of teacher attention;[4] (2) attending to rules and ignoring inappropriate behavior produce either no change or increased inappropriate be-havior; however, when approval for appropriate behavior is added, in-appropriate behavior decreases significantly;[5] (3) manipulation of a teacher's approval and disapproval suggests that the consequences of withdrawing teacher approval and increasing teacher disapproval results in a concomitant increase in disruptive behavior;[6] and (4) negative con-sequation in the form of teacher disapproval may actually function to increase disruptive behavior in the classroom.[7]

Another consequence of how a teacher interacts with students in-volves mistakes of reinforcement. "Mistakes of reinforcement" refers to inconsistency in responding: The teacher either approves of a student's inappropriate behavior or disapproves of appropriate student behavior. Often a teacher sets up rules and then breaks these same rules, thus reinforcing inappropriate behavior. An example of this reinforcement error would be to call on students whose hands are not raised when the rule "Raise your hands if you want to speak" has been previously specified. It has been found that student off-task behavior increases dramatically when a teacher is inconsistent.[8]

Third, it is important to observe the effect magnitude or the inten-sity of reinforcement has in combination with approval and disapproval delivery. Results of studies concerning one aspect of magnitude or inten-sity, loud versus soft reprimands, demonstrated that disruptive behavior increases when the teacher gives loud reprimands and decreases when soft reprimands (which could be heard only by the student being repri-manded) were given.[9]

Perhaps the definitive statement on the intensity or magnitude of teacher behavior when working with small children is that of En-glemann:

The primary reinforcing emphasis was on positive reinforcement. The teacher used herself as a model, 'I'm smart. I can do this stuff.' She used other children in the group as models. 'Did you hear Sidney? He and I are the only ones who can do this. We're smart.' She always tried to acknowledge the correct response of every child in the group. 'Hey, everybody did it that time. Boy, you are smart kids. Good work, Tyrone. You too, Lisa.'

Whenever the teacher taught, she utilized some of the reinforcing techniques. . . . She moved quickly so that the children were not confronted with a static presentation. She spoke loudly one moment, softly the next. She presented interesting examples of the concept when the interesting aspects of the objects did not interfere with the concept being taught. She structured the presentation so that the children had a pay off.[10]

The importance of physical interaction (tugging on an arm to get attention, for example), dramatic change of pace, dynamic presentation of objects, and variation in the volume of the teacher's voice—all exaggeration and intensification of behavior—are stressed by Englemann for the effective teacher.

Finally, observing the effect of teacher reinforcement on appropriate and inappropriate student behavior is important. Research demonstrates a ratio of 80% approval to 20% disapproval is very effective in maintaining on-task academic and social student behavior. Also, it has been observed that the average classroom can tolerate about 20% off-task behavior and still be considered a "good" class.[11]

Results of previous research concerning general classroom teacher behavior demonstrate the importance of overt behavior, or behavior which can be observed, in effecting the best learning environment for students. Data demonstrates that the most successful teachers (1) establish classroom rules and contingencies for both social and academic behavior; (2) act in an approving way toward appropriate student behavior for about 80% of the total social reinforcement frequency; (3) act in a negative or disapproving way toward inappropriate student behavior for only 20% of the total reinforcement frequency; (4) never make errors of reinforcement, i.e., approve of inappropriate behavior or disapprove of appropriate behavior; and (5) use dramatic elements such as high intensity, rapid change of pace, and exaggeration in their teaching.

In music education we are concerned with two general aspects of behavior: attention to a stimulus (music) and a response to it (composing, performing, listening, verbalizing, conceptualizing, and using music for extramusical purposes). It must again be emphasized that the purpose of these observation field experiences is to promote the development of a positive approach to teaching music. The efficacy of a positive approach has been demonstrated not only through research in the general classroom but also through research in music classrooms and rehearsals.

Furthermore, research in music indicates the importance of "music as its own reward" which concerns amounts of time spent in performance versus nonperformance or other use of rehearsal time and dynamic nonverbal conductor behavior.

Throughout these observations, your attention will be directed to the use of approval, disapproval, and mistakes of reinforcement. Behavioral studies in music have shown that music teachers trained in high approval techniques have more attentive students who follow class rules for social behavior better than other groups.[12] In addition, students in band and choral rehearsals appear to have more favorable attitudes toward the music, rehearsals, and conductors when the conductors are highly approving[13] as well as dynamic.[14] Another important study found that students receiving music listening lessons under conditions of high adult approval selected more of that music than student taught under low adult approval conditions.[15]

Although the specific use of rehearsal and class time has not been clearly isolated as a variable in previous research studies, it appears that time spent performing as opposed to not performing functions as a powerful reinforcer independent of the teacher or conductor.[16] Early experimental research demonstrated that both students receiving pennies for appropriate music responses and those not receiving pennies improved significantly in vocal intonation.[17] In a partial replication of that study, sixth grade students were divided into four different reinforcement groups for vocal pitch accuracy. One group was reinforced with listening to rock music; another received two minutes listening to records from a traditional music series; a third, pennies; and the fourth, no reinforcement. There was significant improvement from the pre- to posttests in vocal pitch accuracy scores for *all* groups.[18] Although influencing social behavior, neither the ratio of approval to disapproval of conductor responses nor the magnitude of conductor behavior appear to affect the *academic* performance level of high school choral groups.[19]

In addition to approval/disapproval reinforcement and use of rehearsal time, data from early research on conductor behavior indicate that conductors who exaggerate their overt behaviors or who are dramatic and dynamic can more easily shape favorable attitudes towards music, the rehearsal, and themselves.[20] Exaggerated behaviors include: a high frequency of both group and individual eye contact; body movement toward the group; contrasting approval/disapproval facial expressions; variability in speech speed, voice volume, and pitch; and a high frequency of teaching or shouting reinforcements during group performance.

In summary, it would seem that music teachers and conductors who are most successful in maintaining attentive classes or performing groups, eliciting high levels of achievement or performance, and establishing favorable attitudes toward music, have several observable characteristics in common. First, they are usually highly approving. Second, they dispense approval and disapproval in a very dramatic way by maintaining eye contact, using body movement and contrasting facial expressions, and conducting in an expressive way. Finally, they are efficient users of class and rehearsal time.

Through systematic observation of music classes and rehearsals one may begin to understand the relationship between these characteristics of teacher/conductor behavior and student attentiveness, performance, and attitude. For example, did the altos miss that entrance because the conductor did not maintain eye contact, use an expressive left-hand cueing gesture, and lean towards them? Were students in that kindergarten class off-task because the music teacher made mistakes of reinforcement? Did that junior high band stay 95% on-task because the conductor was highly approving, kept the rehearsal moving at a rapid pace by changing the activity (instruction, group performance, sectional performance) often, and used dramatic overt behavior?

Again it must be emphasized that the purpose of systematic observation is to enhance vicarious learning or modeling. Hopefully through observation new teaching behaviors will be acquired and successful ones will be reinforced.

FIELD EXPERIENCES IN OBSERVATION

1. Learning Systematic Observation Techniques

a. Preparing for Observation

Systematic behavioral observation is meant to sensitize the beginning teacher to those overt demonstrable behaviors of both teacher and students which affect the academic and social behavior of others. Learning to "look" is most important in teaching. Many problems can be avoided by the teacher who is skillful in student observation. Also, creative techniques in classroom management can be learned through observation of skilled professionals.

The following general instructions for observers are quoted from the expanded second edition for professionals of *Teaching/Discipline: A Positive Approach for Educational Development:*[21]

  1. Wear sunglasses when observing. This signals teachers, students, and others that you will not interact with them. During the time of the observation there should be *no* talking or interaction with the teacher, and

questions or recording problems should be settled before entering the classroom whenever possible. If teacher interactions become necessary, make certain that the sunglasses are removed and that observations cease for a short time. Should a teacher initiate interaction during an observation, generally ignore it until the observation is concluded.

2. Sit silently and as immobile as possible when observing. Change location quietly and only when absolutely necessary. If you are observing a particular student or students who change locations, then you may have to change if you are unable to hear the verbal interactions.

3. Your goal as an observer is to become a piece of furniture. Take great care that you do not become a reinforcement variable with reference to the behavior of students or teachers in the classroom.

4. Make no differential responses to students, i.e., laughing at wise-cracks, answering questions directed toward you, smiling at student's responses, or changing position of head or eyes when addressed. Make the minimal movement necessary to see the student, teacher, or other person you are recording. Social behaviors by students either on entering or leaving the classroom or the school should be ignored as well as behaviors directed toward you while you are in the halls. Remember, if ever you decide to talk to another observer, the teacher, or your supervisor, then please remove your glasses.

5. Discussion of any student, by name or otherwise, except with proper school personnel or your immediate supervisor, is a breach of professional conduct.

6. Please conform to the general dress standards of the school so that your dress does not become a variable and/or interfere with the task of observation.

7. During recording intervals, look only at observation forms and attempt to ignore any noises from the person or persons observed.

8. Main objective is for two people watching the same behavior to agree that the same behaviors occurred (reliability). Therefore, remain unsubjective and unbiased as possible at all times. Record what the person does without trying to think what you think he should have done. Your time will come.[22]

b. Observation Procedures

Recording procedures are described as follows:

During the first interval of each time period (ten-second observing and recording intervals have been found to be most useful), the observer should observe and mentally note the ongoing behavior. Observers *do not record the behavior observed at this time.* During the second interval, the behavior observed during the first interval is recorded (marked) on the data sheet. Comments regarding general classroom interaction and/or descriptions of behavior should also be recorded during this time. No observation of behaviors occurs during the second interval as this time period is devoted to recording. Observations are continued during the third interval, but are not recorded until the fourth. The same procedure is followed with the fifth and sixth intervals. Thus behavior is observed during the first, third, and fifth intervals and is recorded during the second, fourth, and sixth. Two or more *different* behaviors may be recorded during any one ten-second interval, but, unless specific directions are given to the contrary, only one symbol of the same behavior should appear in each interval box. After observation expertise has progressed (to .80 reliability), behaviors occurring twice during the same interval can be recorded for the appropriate symbol by using numbers or additional marks. All occurrences should be checked or marked in a conspicuous manner. Colored pencils are excellent for this.[23]

If you are observing a "live" classroom or rehearsal situation, you will need a watch with a sweep hand or second hand so that you can order your observation and recording intervals properly.

Another way to order your observation is to make a cassette tape which says the following:

> Behavioral Observation Forms. Get ready to observe. Line One. Observe—(Pause 10 seconds)—Record—(Pause 5 seconds)—Observe— (Pause 10 seconds)—Record—(Pause 5 seconds)—Observe—(Pause 10 seconds)—Record—(Pause 5 seconds)—Observe—(Pause 10 seconds)— Record—(Pause 5 seconds)—Line Two. Observe—(Pause 10 seconds)— Record—(Pause 5 seconds), etc. through the number of lines on the observation form. At the end of the last line on the observation form, say "Take a new Data Sheet. Get ready to observe. Line One. Observe—" etc. At the end of the *second* complete observe-record sequence, say "End of Observation."

This procedure can structure as many lines (minutes) of observation as needed. The cassette tape should be heard through an earphone so that the observe-record cues will not distract the class in which you are observing.

Generally each line or "time" of observation on the forms within this book represents one minute of clock-time. Therefore the number of seconds allotted for "observing" and "recording" may vary. The following are suggestions for the number of seconds to allot to observation and recording for the forms in this manual:

Student Observation Form C (Figure 3-1)	Observe Interval = 15 seconds Record Interval = 5 seconds (17 lines or minutes)
Teacher Observation Form A (Figures 3-3 and 3-4)	Observe Interval = 15 seconds Record Interval = 5 seconds (17 lines or minutes)

Choral/Instrumental Rehearsal Observation Forms (Figures 3-6 and 3-7)	Observe Interval = 10 seconds Record Interval = 5 seconds (8 lines or minutes)
Music Conductor Observation Form (Figure 3-8)	Observe Interval = 10 seconds Record Interval = 5 seconds (8 lines or minutes)
Elementary Music Teaching Evaluation Form (Figure 3-5)	No cassette tape necessary. Observation is continual rather than time-sampled. (variable time limit)

You may wish to use variable Observe/Record intervals. Although this is acceptable, you may discover that your observations are either becoming too long or too short and must adjust accordingly.

2. Observation in the Regular Classroom

a. Recording Student Behavior

Classroom behavioral observation focusing on the student is concerned with two major kinds of behavior: (1) on-task or appropriate behavior, and (2) off-task or inappropriate behavior. However, students' behavior can be appropriate or inappropriate only with reference to classroom rules and/or to the teacher's objectives. Therefore, observers must know the rules of the classroom and differing rules for specific situations before reliable observations can be recorded. It is sometimes necessary to ask teachers what their rules are.

The following Student Observation Form (see figure 3-1) has been developed to assist you in observing, recording, and analyzing behaviors described in the child categories below.[24] You may also wish to use this form as you participate in the field experience concerning "Designing and Managing Musical Learning" (see Chapter Four). Most student teachers find that inappropriate social behavior is their greatest challenge. Indeed, most resignations from the teaching profession occur from the inability to cope with discipline problems. Through systematic observation and recording of "problem" behaviors followed by specification of the *exact* behaviors and their magnitude, you may develop a clearer definition of the nature of the discipline problem. Then through the process of pinpointing, recording, consequating, and evaluating you may find the task of disciplining easier.

The following definitions of child on-task and off-task categories will help you observe and record specific student behavior using the Student Observation Form (see figure 3-1):

Child Categories

On-Task
+

This category includes verbal and motor behavior that follows the classroom rules and is appropriate to the learning situation. On-task behavior is defined with reference to both the rules of the classroom and the teacher-designated academic activity. If a student is working on the appropriate academic activity and is obeying the rules of the classroom, then the student's behavior is recorded as being on-task. Examples of on-task behavior might include sitting at desk while working, engaging in group games when appropriate, responding to teacher questions (whether or not the answer is correct or incorrect), walking to chalkboard when asked, demonstrating activities to others when expected, talking during class discussions, or participating actively in physical education class.

Off-Task

N

Verbal Noise

Verbal noise is any oral response that breaks the class rules and/or interrupts the learning situation. This category may include inappropriate talking, yelling, blurting out, whistling, humming, screaming, singing, and laughing. The verbalization must be heard for it to be recorded. Simply seeing the student's lips move is not enough. If a child responds to a teacher's question of instruction, then the student is on-task. Further examples of verbal off-task behavior include blurting out an answer instead of raising hand, talking to a neighbor instead of working on materials, and singing during discussion.

Object Noise

Object noise is any audible noise resulting from any behavior on the part of the child that may cause other children to be off-task, such as slamming books, kicking furniture, or rapping a desk.

M

Motor

Motor off-task is any motor response (gross or minor) that breaks the class rules and/or interrupts the learning situation. Some motor behaviors are inappropriate during certain classroom periods but not always at others.

Gross Motor

Gross motor behaviors may include getting out of one's seat, turning around at least 90°, running, turning cartwheels, walking around the room, waving arms. Another area of inappropriate gross motor behavior includes behaviors generally labelled "aggressive"—hitting, kicking, pushing, pinching, slapping, striking another person with objects, grabbing another's property, and throwing.

Minor Motor

Minor motor behaviors are only recorded when attention is not directed toward the student's work. If the student is engaged in appropriate activities while he exhibits these small motor behaviors, then this behavior is recorded as being on-task with a check mark in "M" and mention is made of these motor activities in the comment section. Examples of minor motor behaviors include thumbsucking, fingernail biting, fiddling with hair, finger twiddling, chewing on a pencil or other object, and playing with learning materials when not appropriate.

O   ### Other or Passive Off-Task

The student is involved in no interaction or is doing nothing when expected to be involved. Behaviors recorded in this category include daydreaming and staring into space. The student must be engaged in no motor or verbal activity for this category to be recorded. It is important to remember that there are times when doing nothing is not inappropriate, for example, when an assignment is completed and nothing has been assigned. This is very rare as most teachers have activities for all students when one assignment is completed.[25]

b. Recording Teacher Behavior

Research shows that the more contingent teachers are in the classroom, the more successful they are in promoting appropriate academic and social behavior. Therefore, the development of a contingent and positive approach to teaching becomes important in structuring for more efficient and effective teaching.

When observing teacher reinforcement in the classroom using the Teacher Observation Form (see figures 3-3 and 3-4),[26] remember that reinforcement must follow student behavior. Encouraging students or giving directions may stimulate student behavior but is not considered reinforcement of that behavior because the stimulus comes *before* the behavior. The following rehearsal situation clarifies this difference:

STUDENT OBSERVATION - FORM C

Observer ______________________ Student ______________________

Reliability Observer ______________________ Teacher ______________________

No. in class or group ______________________ Grade or Subject ______________ Date ______________

General Activity ______________________ Time: Start ______________ End ______________

Observation Interval ______________ (seconds) Page ______________ of ______________

Record Interval ______________ (seconds)

		INTERVALS						
TIME	ACTIVITY CODE	(1)	2-Record	(3)	4-Record	(5)	6-Record	Comments
1		Observe Now	+ N M O	Observe Now	+ N M O	Observe Now	+ N M O	
2			+ N M O		+ N M O		+ N M O	
3			+ N M O		+ N M O		+ N M O	
4			+ N M O		+ N M O		+ N M O	
5			+ N M O		+ N M O		+ N M O	
6		Observe Now	+ N M O	Observe Now	+ N M O	Observe Now	+ N M O	
7			+ N M O		+ N M O		+ N M O	
8			+ N M O		+ N M O		+ N M O	
9			+ N M O		+ N M O		+ N M O	
10			+ N M O		+ N M O		+ N M O	
11		Observe Now	+ N M O	Observe Now	+ N M O	Observe Now	+ N M O	
12			+ N M O		+ N M O		+ N M O	
13			+ N M O		+ N M O		+ N M O	
14			+ N M O		+ N M O		+ N M O	
15		Observe Now	+ N M O	Observe Now	+ N M O	Observe Now	+ N M O	
16			+ N M O		+ N M O		+ N M O	
17			+ N M O		+ N M O			

% On-task = ______________ (+%)

% Off-task = 100 - (% On-task) = ______________

Totals:		Intervals Observed		
+ =	______ -	______	=	______ %
N =	______ -	______	=	______ %
M =	______ -	______	=	______ %
0 =	______ -	______	=	______ %

Figure 3-1 [*Madsen and Madsen,* Teaching/Discipline, *p. 250.*]

Band Director: Sit up straight, flutes!   (stimulus)
                 [Flutes sit up straight.]   (student behavior)
Band Director: That's it, flutes. Good posture!   (reinforcement)

A simple way to analyze reinforcement categories is to study the following 2 × 2 contingency table (see figure 3-2):

TEACHER BEHAVIOR

		Approval	Disapproval
STUDENT BEHAVIOR	APPROPRIATE (Social & Academic)	As Aa (Box 1)	(Ds) (Da) (Mistakes) (Box 2)
	INAPPROPRIATE (Social & Academic)	(As) (Aa) (Mistakes) (Box 3)	Ds Da Unless Payoff (Box 4)

Figure 3-2 Behavioral Contingency Interaction Table*

Student behavior is categorized as either appropriate or inappropriate while teacher reinforcement for student behavior may be either approving or disapproving. These behavioral contingency interactions are explained as follows (refer to figure 3-2 as you read):

When a teacher follows a behavior with approval, this may serve to reinforce the appropriate behavior (Box 1: When you do good things, good things happen to you). When a teacher gives approval following inappropriate behavior, this is regarded as a reinforcement mistake which may increase the rate of inappropriate behavior! This is called an *approval mistake* (Box 3: When you do bad things, good things happen to you).

Disapproval when properly used generally serves to stop or decrease the rate of the disapproved behavior (Box 4: When you do bad things, bad things happen to you). Therefore, the teacher may be making a mistake if disapproval follows appropriate behavior. This is called a disapproval mistake (Box 2: When you do good things, bad things happen to you).

Disapproval following inappropriate behavior is intended to decrease the inappropriate behavior (Box 4). But, if the student has learned an improper association, the disapproval may function in a different way, depending upon the reinforcement history of the student. Teacher attention may also be reinforcing and students may work for whatever attention is forthcoming—even disapproval. Disapproving behavior alone without approval for appropriate behavior will often increase the very behavior that the teacher wishes to eliminate. In the lower half of Box 4, the attention serves as a payoff. The

Madsen and Madsen, Teaching/Discipline, *p. 242.*

upper half of Box 4 shows occasional disapproval is strong enough to stop inappropriate behavior. (When you do bad things, bad things happen to you.) The effects of disapproval following any student behavior probably depend upon the amount of approval to appropriate behavior (Box 1) in relation to the amount of disapproval to inappropriate behavior (Box 4). When the teacher uses more approval to appropriate behavior than disapproval to inappropriate, then both are generally more effective. The contrast between approval and disapproval also serves to enhance the effect of both. When the teacher uses only approval, then students learn that no matter what one does, "good things" happen. When the teacher uses only disapproval, the students learn that no matter what they do, "bad things" happen to them.[27]

The following Teacher Observation Form (see figure 3-3) has been developed to assist you in observing, recording, and analyzing approvals, disapprovals, and mistakes of reinforcement as described above. Before beginning your observation, you might review approval/disapproval responses available to teachers within the five categories listed in *Teaching/Discipline:* words, spoken or written; physical expressions, facial or bodily; closeness, nearness, or touching; activities, social or individual; and things, materials, food, awards, or tokens.[28] As you observe you will notice that the best teachers have a very large approval/disapproval reinforcement repertory.

Teacher observation categories for the development of a positive approach to teaching include the following:

Teacher Observation Categories

Aa — Approval for academic behavior is recorded if the teacher indicates the academic work is correct. Academic approval usually involves words, spoken or written. The observer should watch carefully to determine if physical expressions, closeness, activities, or things are specifically paired with correct answers, indicating attention or commendation for the correct answer rather than the "working" itself. Care should be exercised in discriminating between approval directed toward academic work and approval for correct social behavior.

As — Approval for social behavior is recorded if the teacher gives any approving response paired specifically with appropriate social behavior. This category includes words, physical expressions, closeness, activities, and things directed toward any social behavior (following rules, working, cooperating, getting on-task).

Da — Disapproval for academic behavior includes any disapproval indicating that a student's response to the cur-

TEACHER OBSERVATION - FORM A

Observer_____ Teacher_____
Reliability Observer_____ Grade or Subject_____
No. in Class or Group _____ Date_____
General Activity_____ Time: Start_____ End_____
Length of Observational Intervals in Seconds_____
Record Intervals in Seconds _____ Page_____of_____

TIME	ACTIVITY CODE	(1)	2-RECORD	(3)	4-RECORD	(5)	6-RECORD	COMMENTS
1		OBSERVE NOW	As Aa (Ds) Da / (As)(Aa) Ds Da	OBSERVE NOW	As Aa (Ds) Da / (As)(Aa) Ds Da	OBSERVE NOW	As Aa (Ds) Da / (As)(Aa) Ds Da	
2			As Aa (Ds)(Da) / (As)(Aa) Ds Da		As Aa (Ds)(Da) / (As)(Aa) Ds Da		As Aa (Ds)(Da) / (As)(Aa) Ds Da	
3			As Aa (Ds)(Da) / (As)(Aa) Ds Da		As Aa (Ds)(Da) / (As)(Aa) Ds Da		As Aa (Ds)(Da) / (As)(Aa) Ds Da	
4			As Aa (Ds)(Da) / (As)(Aa) Ds Da		As Aa (Ds)(Da) / (As)(Aa) Ds Da		As Aa (Ds)(Da) / (As)(Aa) Ds Da	
5			As Aa (Ds)(Da) / (As)(Aa) Ds Da		As Aa (Ds)(Da) / (As)(Aa) Ds Da		As Aa (Ds)(Da) / (As)(Aa) Ds Da	
6			As Aa (Ds)(Da) / (As)(Aa) Ds Da		As Aa (Ds)(Da) / (As)(Aa) Ds Da		As Aa (Ds)(Da) / (As)(Aa) Ds Da	
7			As Aa (Ds)(Da) / (As)(Aa) Ds Da		As Aa (Ds)(Da) / (As)(Aa) Ds Da		As Aa (Ds)(Da) / (As)(Aa) Ds Da	
8		OBSERVE NOW	As Aa (Ds)(Da) / (As)(Aa) Ds Da	OBSERVE NOW	As Aa (Ds)(Da) / (As)(Aa) Ds Da	OBSERVE NOW	As Aa (Ds)(Da) / (As)(Aa) Ds Da	
9			As Aa (Ds)(Da) / (As)(Aa) Ds Da		As Aa (Ds)(Da) / (As)(Aa) Ds Da		As Aa (Ds)(Da) / (As)(Aa) Ds Da	
10			As Aa (Ds)(Da) / (As)(Aa) Ds Da		As Aa (Ds)(Da) / (As)(Aa) Ds Da		As Aa (Ds)(Da) / (As)(Aa) Ds Da	
11			As Aa (Ds)(Da) / (As)(Aa) Ds Da		As Aa (Ds)(Da) / (As)(Aa) Ds Da		As Aa (Ds)(Da) / (As)(Aa) Ds Da	
12			As Aa (Ds)(Da) / (As)(Aa) Ds Da		As Aa (Ds)(Da) / (As)(Aa) Ds Da		As Aa (Ds)(Da) / (As)(Aa) Ds Da	
13			As Aa (Ds)(Da) / (As)(Aa) Ds Da		As Aa (Ds)(Da) / (As)(Aa) Ds Da		As Aa (Ds)(Da) / (As)(Aa) Ds Da	
14		OBSERVE NOW	As Aa (Ds)(Da) / (As)(Aa) Ds Da	OBSERVE NOW	As Aa (Ds)(Da) / (As)(Aa) Ds Da	OBSERVE NOW	As Aa (Ds)(Da) / (As)(Aa) Ds Da	
15			As Aa (Ds)(Da) / (As)(Aa) Ds Da		As Aa (Ds)(Da) / (As)(Aa) Ds Da		As Aa (Ds)(Da) / (As)(Aa) Ds Da	
16			As Aa (Ds)(Da) / (As)(Aa) Ds Da		As Aa (Ds)(Da) / (As)(Aa) Ds Da		As Aa (Ds)(Da) / (As)(Aa) Ds Da	
17			As Aa (Ds)(Da) / (As)(Aa) Ds Da		As Aa (Ds)(Da) / (As)(Aa) Ds Da		TOTALS:	

INTERVALS

TOTALS:
As____ Aa____ (Ds)____ (Da)____
(As)____ (Aa)____ Ds____ Da____

Figure 3-3 [*Madsen and Madsen,* Teaching/Discipline, *p. 237.*]

DATA SUMMARY SHEET
TEACHER OBSERVATION FORM A

Social Reinforcement

Symbols Total No. Observed ÷ Total Intervals Observed = % Intervals

                                                       Behavior Observed

As = _____ ÷ _____ = _____ %

Ds = _____ ÷ _____ = _____ %

(As) = _____ ÷ _____ = _____ %

(Ds) = _____ ÷ _____ = _____ %

Social Approval Ratio: $\dfrac{As}{As + Ds + \text{(As)} + \text{(Ds)}}$ (OR) ___ ÷ ___ + ___ + ___ + ___ = ___ %

Academic Reinforcement

Symbols = Total No. Observed ÷ Total Intervals Observed = % Intervals

                                                       Behavior Observed

Aa = _____ ÷ _____ = _____ %

Da = _____ ÷ _____ = _____ %

(Aa) = _____ ÷ _____ = _____ %

(Da) = _____ ÷ _____ = _____ %

Academic Approval Ratio: $\dfrac{Aa}{Aa + Da + \text{(Aa)} + \text{(Da)}}$ (OR) ___ ÷ ___ + ___ + ___ + ___ = ___ %

$$\text{RELIABILITY} = \frac{\text{Total Agree}}{\text{Total Agree + Total Disagree}} = \_\_\_ \%$$

Symbols	Number Observed			Same Symbol in Same Interval	
	Observer I	Reliability	Observer	Agree	Disagree
As	_____	_____		_____	_____
Ds	_____	_____		_____	_____
(As)	_____	_____		_____	_____
(Ds)	_____	_____		_____	_____
Aa	_____	_____		_____	_____
Da	_____	_____		_____	_____
(Aa)	_____	_____		_____	_____
(Da)	_____	_____		_____	_____

Figure 3-4 [*Madsen and Madsen,* Teaching/Discipline, *p. 239.*]

riculum materials was incorrect. Disapproval in classrooms generally involves words, spoken or written (grades), but one should not overlook physical expression, closeness (hitting, grabbing, forcibly holding, putting out of group), or deprivation of activities or things.

Ds

Disapproval for social behavior given by the teacher follows any disruption of the learning environment which interferes with learning. Disapproval includes words, spoken or written, that reprimand. Disapproval may be of either high or low intensity and includes yelling, scolding, threats and threatening comments concerning later consequences. Disapproval also includes bodily expressions such as frowning, grimacing, or shaking a fist, closeness such as hitting, slapping, paddling, or other means of corporal punishment, and deprivation of activities or things. Corporal punishment is *not* advised, yet is sometimes observed and thus is included within observational categories.

(Aa)

An approval mistake of reinforcement following academic behavior occurs when the teacher indicates the academic response is correct when, in fact, the answer is incorrect.

(As)

An approval mistake of reinforcement following social behavior involves giving approval to inappropriate social behavior. For example, a teacher may touch a student "gently" during or following a misbehavior (closeness) or may reinforce the misbehavior through words, bodily expressions, activities, or things. An approval mistake is recorded when the teacher follows a student's breaking of classroom rules with an approval response (inconsistency). The teacher may verbally recognize a student who is walking around when he is supposed to be in his seat, or the teacher may recognize a student who blurts out an answer (whether correct or incorrect) although the student is supposed to raise his hand for recognition. An approval mistake could also occur if the teacher uses words to dispense group verbal approval (praise) when one or more of the students in the group is off-task.

(Da)

A disapproval mistake of reinforcement following academic behavior is recorded when the teacher indicates the student's academic answer was incorrect when the answer was, in fact, correct.

(Ds)

A disapproval mistake of reinforcement following social behavior is recorded if the teacher uses disapproval when the social behavior was indeed appropriate to the classroom situation. This occurs most frequently when the teacher gives group disapproval and one or more of the students are, in fact, on-task. A disapproval mistake may also occur when the teacher interrupts his work with one student in order to attend another student. Interruptions may lead to a disapproval mistake of reinforcement if the student behavior is disapproved in the process. Disapproval mistakes also occur when the teacher delays too long in using disapproval for inappropriate behavior. For example, a student engages in inappropriate behavior, stops the inappropriate behavior, is working appropriately, and then the teacher disapproves.[29]

3. Using Observational Data to Improve Teaching and Learning in Music

a. Observing Elementary Music Classes

The following Elementary Music Teaching Evaluation Form (see figure 3-5) has been developed by Moore[30] to assist in observing elementary classroom music lessons. Space is provided on the form for tallying approvals and disapprovals, determining the reinforcement rate and percentage of approval, and rating student participation and reinforcement effectiveness. In addition to the observation of social behavior and interaction, the form includes academic categories such as musical concept, lesson organization, musical medium, and musicianship which must be specified and rated. Finally, the form includes the category of creativity in which the number of different musical responses made by both teachers and students is counted.

The following are definitions for each category of the Elementary Music Teaching Evaluation Form:

Teacher Interaction (six categories)

Number of Approvals = frequency of positive things the teacher does that encourages student response.

Number of Disapprovals = frequency of negative things the teacher does that discourage student response.

Reinforcement Rate = the sum of approvals and disapprovals divided by the number of minutes taught—i.e., the number of reinforcers per minute ($A + D \div$ time).

Percent of Approvals = the number of approvals divided by the sum of approvals plus disapprovals ($A \div A + D$).

ELEMENTARY MUSIC TEACHING EVALUATION FORM

Teacher_____

Evaluator _____

Point of Evaluation

		Point of Evaluation	
I.	Teacher Interaction	1. Number of Approvals	
		2. Number of Disapprovals	
		3. Reinforcement Rate (A + D ÷ time)	
		4. Percent of Approvals A ÷ (A + D)	
		5. Student Participation*	
		6. Reinforcement Effectiveness*	
II.	Musicianship	7. Specify Musical Concept (pitch, beat, etc.)	
		8. Accuracy of Concept*	
		9. Lesson Organization*	
		10. Specify Musical Medium (voice &/or instrument)	
		11. Quality of Musicianship*	
III.	Creativity	12. Student Creativity**	
		13. Teacher Creativity**	
		14. TOTALS (rows 5,6,8,9,11-13)	
		15. Minutes per Lesson	

```
*   0 = none                **Number of different
  1-2 = bad                   student or teacher
  3-4 = poor                  responses made about
  5-6 = fair                  the musical concept
  7-8 = good                  being taught.
 9-10 = excellent
```

Figure 3-5

Student Participation = value judgment from 0–10, none to excellent, rating the involvement of students in the class being taught.

Reinforcement Effectiveness = rating on the 0–10 scale the efficacy of teacher feedback to student responses.

Musicianship (five categories)

Musical Concept = identify the exact musical idea being taught.

Accuracy of Concept = judge on the 0–10 scale the academic correctness of the musical concept taught.

Lesson Organization = evaluate on the 0–10 scale the sequential teaching procedures as they relate to the concept taught.

Musical Medium = name the musical instrument(s) utilized by the teacher.

Quality of Musicianship = rate the musicianship of the teacher on the 0–10 scale.

Creativity (two categories)

Student Creativity = frequency of different musical responses made by students about the musical concept taught.

Teacher Creativity = frequency of different teacher-initiated music activities related to the musical concept taught.

Totals

To determine a total evaluation rating, the scores for rows 5, 6, 8, 9, and 11–13 are added. An outstanding teacher would achieve a total rating of 50 or more.

Minutes per Lesson = number of minutes utilized in teaching the mini-music lesson.

This form is not to be used with an "observe-record" time-sampled observation sequence. Rather it provides a method of evaluating the lesson as a whole through (a) *counting* various responses throughout the lesson rather than during an "observe" interval, and (b) *rating* various aspects of the lesson immediately following the presentation. The observer is reminded that lines 1, 2, 12, and 13 must be counted *during* the lesson. The remainder of the form can be completed following the lesson.

b. Observing Choral and Instrumental Rehearsals

The Choral and Instrumental Observation forms (see figures 3-6 and 3-7) help you to observe systematically student activity, student on/off-task, and teacher/conductor responses. Observation procedures are identical to those described earlier. Student on/off-task is defined as follows:

On-Task: Active—When a student is supposed to be singing/playing, he must be singing/playing and looking at either the music or teacher.

                   Passive—When student is not supposed to be singing/playing, he must be quiet and looking at either music, teacher, or chorus/band/orchestra members who are singing/playing.

                   Other—Student must follow instructions given by teacher.

Off-Task: Observably not on-task.

It is recommended that only *verbal* approval and disapproval teacher responses be recorded on this form since the Music Conductor Observation Form provides opportunities to observe nonverbal forms of teacher reinforcement. Verbal approval responses include comments like: "Good," "That's right, basses!" "Altos, you're really with it today," "Beautiful tone, flutes!" "Nice phrasing!" Disapproval verbal responses include comments like: "You're always late!" "Follow me, not your neighbor!" "Sit up straight. Don't slouch." "No! Wrong again!" "Too loud!" "Terrible! You're playing so flat, I can't tell what the tune is!"

Student and teacher/conductor behavior should be recorded every 15 seconds (10-second observe interval/5-second record interval) in one of the boxes on the form:

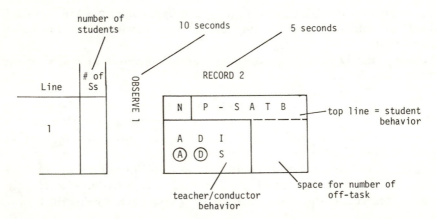

The top line (see above = N P - S A T B) concerns student performance behavior. The section below and to the left of the student performance line concerns teacher/conductor verbal behavior (see above = A D I - Ⓐ Ⓓ S).   The blank space to the right of this is where the observer should record the number of students off-task (see above).

Time used for performance (P), nonperformance (N), and section

CHORAL REHEARSAL OBSERVATION FORM:

Student Activity; Student On/Off-Task; Teacher Response

Observer_____ School _____
Reliability Observer_____ Teacher _____
Number in Group_____ Group Name _____
Time: Start _____End_____ Selection(s)_____
Page _____ of _____ Observe/Record Interval_____

INTERVALS

Line	# of Ss	OBSERVE 1	RECORD 2	OBSERVE 3	RECORD 4	OBSERVE 5	RECORD 6	OBSERVE 7	RECORD 8	Comments
1			N P - S A T B / A D I / Ⓐ Ⓓ S		N P - S A T B / A D I / Ⓐ Ⓓ S		N P - S A T B / A D I / Ⓐ Ⓓ S		N P - S A T B / A D I / Ⓐ Ⓓ S	
2			N P - S A T B / A D I / Ⓐ Ⓓ S		N P - S A T B / A D I / Ⓐ Ⓓ S		N P - S A T B / A D I / Ⓐ Ⓓ S		N P - S A T B / A D I / Ⓐ Ⓓ S	
3			N P - S A T B / A D I / Ⓐ Ⓓ S		N P - S A T B / A D I / Ⓐ Ⓓ S		N P - S A T B / A D I / Ⓐ Ⓓ S		N P - S A T B / A D I / Ⓐ Ⓓ S	
4			N P - S A T B / A D I / Ⓐ Ⓓ S		N P - S A T B / A D I / Ⓐ Ⓓ S		N P - S A T B / A D I / Ⓐ Ⓓ S		N P - S A T B / A D I / Ⓐ Ⓓ S	
5			N P - S A T B / A D I / Ⓐ Ⓓ S		N P - S A T B / A D I / Ⓐ Ⓓ S		N P - S A T B / A D I / Ⓐ Ⓓ S		N P - S A T B / A D I / Ⓐ Ⓓ S	
6			N P - S A T B / A D I / Ⓐ Ⓓ S		N P - S A T B / A D I / Ⓐ Ⓓ S		N P - S A T B / A D I / Ⓐ Ⓓ S		N P - S A T B / A D I / Ⓐ Ⓓ S	
7			N P - S A T B / A D I / Ⓐ Ⓓ S		N P - S A T B / A D I / Ⓐ Ⓓ S		N P - S A T B / A D I / Ⓐ Ⓓ S		N P - S A T B / A D I / Ⓐ Ⓓ S	
8			N P - S A T B / A D I / Ⓐ Ⓓ S		N P - S A T B / A D I / Ⓐ Ⓓ S		N P - S A T B / A D I / Ⓐ Ⓓ S		N P - S A T B / A D I / Ⓐ Ⓓ S	

TOTALS:

N intervals _____   A_____   I _____   % off-task _____
P intervals _____   Ⓐ_____   S   % on-task _____
Section intervals _____ D_____
  (SATB combinations)   Ⓓ_____   Other _____   Reliability_____

_____ _____   Reliability _____

Reliability _____   Reliability _____

Figure 3-6

INSTRUMENTAL REHEARSAL OBSERVATION FORM

Student Activity; Student On/Off Task; Teacher Response

Observer______________________________ School______________________________
Reliability Observer______________________ Teacher______________________________
Number in Group __________ Group Name ____________________________
Time: Start ______ End ______ Selection(s) ____________________________
Page ______ of ______ Observe/Record Interval__________________

INTERVALS

Line	# of Ss	OBSERVE 1	Band Sections: I RECORD 2	OBSERVE 3	II RECORD 4	OBSERVE 5	III RECORD 6	OBSERVE 7	IV RECORD 8
1			N P I II III IV A D I Ⓐ Ⓓ 0		N P I II III IV A D I Ⓐ Ⓓ 0		N P I II III IV A D I Ⓐ Ⓓ 0		N P I II III IV A D I Ⓐ Ⓓ 0
2			N P I II III IV A D I Ⓐ Ⓓ 0		N P I II III IV A D I Ⓐ Ⓓ 0		N P I II III IV A D I Ⓐ Ⓓ 0		N P I II III IV A D I Ⓐ Ⓓ 0
3			N P I II III IV A D I Ⓐ Ⓓ 0		N P I II III IV A D I Ⓐ Ⓓ 0		N P I II III IV A D I Ⓐ Ⓓ 0		N P I II III IV A D I Ⓐ Ⓓ 0
4			N P I II III IV A D I Ⓐ Ⓓ 0		N P I II III IV A D I Ⓐ Ⓓ 0		N P I II III IV A D I Ⓐ Ⓓ 0		N P I II III IV A D I Ⓐ Ⓓ 0
5			N P I II III IV A D I Ⓐ Ⓓ 0		N P I II III IV A D I Ⓐ Ⓓ 0		N P I II III IV A D I Ⓐ Ⓓ 0		N P I II III IV A D I Ⓐ Ⓓ 0
6			N P I II III IV A D I Ⓐ Ⓓ 0		N P I II III IV A D I Ⓐ Ⓓ 0		N P I II III IV A D I Ⓐ Ⓓ 0		N P I II III IV A D I Ⓐ Ⓓ 0
7			N P I II III IV A D I Ⓐ Ⓓ 0		N P I II III IV A D I Ⓐ Ⓓ 0		N P I II III IV A D I Ⓐ Ⓓ 0		N P I II III IV A D I Ⓐ Ⓓ 0
8			N P I II III IV A D I Ⓐ Ⓓ 0		N P I II III IV A D I Ⓐ Ⓓ 0		N P I II III IV A D I Ⓐ Ⓓ 0		N P I II III IV A D I Ⓐ Ⓓ 0

TOTALS: N intervals ______ A ______
P intervals ______ Ⓐ ______
Section intervals ______ D ______
% on task ______ Ⓓ ______
% off task ______ I ______
0 ______

SECTIONS:

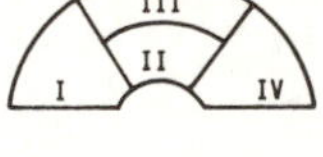

Figure 3-7

rehearsals (S A T B; I II III IV) can be recorded using the following categories of behavior:

Teacher

I = Instruction	Giving verbal directions concerning the music, performing an example, asking and answering questions concerning the music or its performance. Also, the accompanist may be performing an example.
S = Singing	Singing or speaking in ensemble with students.
O = Other	Other teacher responses not fitting above categories, e.g., long pauses, jokes, or verbalizations not concerning music or its performance.
A = Approval	Any verbal endorsement of an appropriate rehearsal behavior.
(A)=Approval Error	Any verbal approval of an inappropriate rehearsal behavior. Reinforcement mistake.
D = Disapproval	Verbal reprimand of an inappropriate rehearsal behavior.
(D)=Disapproval Error	Any verbal disapproval of an appropriate rehearsal behavior. Reinforcement mistake.

Student

N =Nonperformance	Chorus/band/orchestra is not singing/playing during the majority of the observation interval.
P = Performance	Entire chorus/band/orchestra is singing/playing/speaking in ensemble during the majority of the interval. Mutually exclusive from "N."
S–A–T–B I–II–III–IV	Section(s) is (are) singing/speaking/playing during the majority of the observation interval. These categories are mutually exclusive from "P" and "N" but *not* from each other.

Each form requires 8 minutes to complete. It is recommended that a 16-minute (or two forms) rehearsal segment be observed and recorded.

If the group under observation is large (40–100 singers or players), it will probably be necessary for the observer to divide them either by section (SATB) or by row for counting off-task behavior. In this instance, the observer would divide the blank space in each square on the observation form provided for recording the number of students off-task as follows:

| Record total number of students observed here | Record number of students off-task here |

After observations are completed, totals should be entered at the bottom of the form. Spaces are provided for the number of N intervals, P intervals, approvals, disapprovals, etc., on both the Choral and Instrumental Observation Forms. Also, percentage of off-task can be computed using the following formula:

$$\frac{\text{number of students off-task}}{\text{total number of students}}$$

The total number of students (the denominator in the above formula) may be added in two ways depending on the method of observation. If one has observed the group as a whole, the number of students observed in each interval will be the same. Therefore, the total number of students would be: the number of students × the number of intervals (32). However, if the group has been divided into sections for the purpose of off-task observation, the total number of students observed may be different for each interval: e.g., there may be 14 sopranos, 12 altos, 8 tenors, and 12 basses; thus, the number of students in each interval would have to be added together to get the total number of students.

c. Observing Conductor Behavior

The Music Conductor Observation Form (see figures 3-8 and 3-9) should be used to observe nonverbal conducting behavior such as body movement, conducting gesture, eye contact, and facial expressions. Also, data can be collected on verbal behaviors, e.g., instruction, singing or teaching during performance, voice pitch, speed, and volume.

Operational definitions for each category on the form are as follows:

Activity	I—	Instructing. Conductor has stopped group performance and is demonstrating or giving instructions.
	SP—	Singing or chanting rhythm while group is performing.
	TP—	Teaching or talking while group is performing. This includes instructions as well as one-word reinforcements, e.g., "Good."
Body Movement	A—	Approaching group. Motion can be side to side, leaning in direction of group at a 45° angle, or walk-

MUSIC CONDUCTOR OBSERVATION FORM

Observer_____ Teacher_____ School_____

Reliability Observer_____ Number in group_____ Selection(s)_____

Time: Start_____ End_____ Date_____ Page_____ of_____

		Activity	Body Movement	Conducting Gestures	Eye Contact	Facial Expressions	Speech Speed	Voice Pitch	Voice Volume
LINE 1	1	I SP TP	A D S	S E None	G I M O	A D N	S H R	L V H	S N L
	2	I SP TP	A D S	S E None	G I M O	A D N	S H R	L V H	S N L
	3	I SP TP	A D S	S E None	G I M O	A D N	S H R	L V H	S N L
	4	I SP TP	A D S	S E None	G I M O	A D N	S H R	L V H	S N L
LINE 2	5	I SP TP	A D S	S E None	G I M O	A D N	S H R	L V H	S N L
	6	_ SP TP	A D S	S E None	G I M O	A D N	S H R	L V H	S N L
	7	I SP TP	A D S	S E None	G I M O	A D N	S H R	L V H	S N L
	8	I SP TP	A D S	S E None	G I M O	A D N	S H R	L V H	S N L
LINE 3	9	I SP TP	A D S	S E None	G I M O	A D N	S H R	L V H	S N L
	10	I SP TP	A D S	S E None	G I M O	A D N	S H R	L V H	S N L
	11	I SP TP	A D S	S E None	G I M O	A D N	S H R	L V H	S N L
	12	I SP TP	A D S	S E None	G I M O	A D N	S H R	L V H	S N L
LINE 4	13	I SP TP	A D S	S E None	G I M O	A D N	S H R	L V H	S N L
	14	I SP TP	A D S	S E None	G I M O	A D N	S H R	L V H	S N L
	15	I SP TP	A D S	S E None	G I M O	A D N	S H R	L V H	S N L
	16	I SP TP	A D S	S E None	G I M O	A D N	S H R	L V H	S N L
LINE 5	17	I SP TP	A D S	S E None	G I M O	A D N	S H R	L V H	S N L
	18	I SP TP	A D S	S E None	G I M O	A D N	S H R	L V H	S N L
	19	I SP TP	A D S	S E None	G I M O	A D N	S H R	L V H	S N L
	20	I SP TP	A D S	S E None	G I M O	A D N	S H R	L V H	S N L
LINE 6	21	I SP TP	A D S	S E None	G I M O	A D N	S H R	L V H	S N L
	22	I SP TP	A D S	S E None	G I M O	A D N	S H R	L V H	S N L
	23	I SP TP	A D S	S E None	G I M O	A D N	S H R	L V H	S N L
	24	I SP TP	A D S	S E None	G I M O	A D N	S H R	L V H	S N L
LINE 7	25	I SP TP	A D S	S E None	G I M O	A D N	S H R	L V H	S N L
	26	I SP TP	A D S	S E None	G I M O	A D N	S H R	L V H	S N L
	27	I SP TP	A D S	S E None	G I M O	A D N	S H R	L V H	S N L
	28	I SP TP	A D S	S E None	G I M O	A D N	S H R	L V H	S N L
LINE 8	29	I SP TP	A D S	S E None	G I M O	A D N	S H R	L V H	S N L
	30	I SP TP	A D S	S E None	G I M O	A D N	S H R	L V H	S N L
	31	I SP TP	A D S	S E None	G I M O	A D N	S H R	L V H	S N L
	32	I SP TP	A D S	S E None	G I M O	A D N	S H R	L V H	S N L

Mannerisms (foot tapping, bouncing, facial tics, over-
use of certain words, clapping hands, finger   _____
snapping, touching face, hair, glasses with hands, _____
mouthing words, adjusting clothing, etc.):
Also, list frequency of occurence.   _____

Comments: _____
_____

Figure 3-8

MUSIC CONDUCTOR OBSERVATION FORM
DATA SUMMARY SHEET

Activity: I _____

             SP _____

             TP _____

Body Movement: A _____

                    D _____

                    S _____

Conducting
Gestures: S _____

             E _____

     None _____

Eye Contact: G _____

                I _____

                M _____

                O _____

Facial Expressions: A _____

                        D _____

                        N _____

Speech Speed: S _____

                H _____

                R _____

Voice Pitch: L _____

              V _____

              H _____

Voice Volume: S _____

                N _____

                L _____

Categories which need
  Improvement

_____

_____

_____

_____

_____

Kind of Improvement

_____

_____

_____

_____

_____

Figure 3-9

ing forward. Several occurrences could be noted only once per interval.

D— Departure from group. Usually a return to a central position behind music stand. Walking backwards or leaning backwards. Several occurrences should be noted only once per interval.

S— Stationary. Conductor stays behind music stand or stands still. Mark "S" only if conductor is stationary for the entire interval.

Conducting Gestures

S— Strict. Conductor moves hands and arms in strict beat pattern. No variation in size of pattern.

E— Expressive. Any deviation from strict beat pattern for purposes of indicating dynamics, phrasing, etc. Variations in size of pattern.

None—Mark "None" only if conductor is not conducting during the *entire* interval.

Eye Contact

G— Conductor is looking at entire group or section for at least three continuous seconds.

I— Conductor is looking at individual in group or accompanist for at least three continuous seconds.

M— Conductor is looking at music for at least three continuous seconds.

O— Conductor is looking at something other than group, individuals, or music, e.g., ceiling, floor. Mark "O" only if it occurs for the entire interval.

Facial Expressions

A— Conductor's face expresses approval by smiling, grinning, raised eyebrows, winking, opening and widening eyes, nodding head up and down.

D— Conductor's face expresses disapproval by frowning, knitted eyebrows, looking at ceiling, smirking, wrinkling mouth, squinting eyes, wrinkling forehead or nose, puckering lips, grimacing, tightening jaw or lips, twisting side of mouth, raising lips.

N— Conductor's face is neutral mask. No expressions which can be interpreted as approval/disapproval. No frowns, smiles, etc. Mark "N" only if expression is neutral for the entire interval.

Note: For categories "Speech Speed," "Voice Pitch," and "Voice Volume," if conductor is *singing* or not *speaking,* leave interval blank. It is recommended that the observer observe voice categories last. This will allow the observer to become well acquainted with the pitch variations of the conductor's speaking voice as well as variations in voice volume.

Speech Speed	S—	Steady. Constant flow of words without pause or repetition. Also, one-word commands or reinforcements, e.g., "Good."
	H—	Hesitant. Pausing between words, "uh's."
	R—	Repetitive. Repetition of words or phrases, i.e., "That's it basses, that's it," or "page 24 . . . page 24."
	Note:	It is possible to have more than one of these (S, H, or R) occur within any interval, e.g., conductor may speak steadily for five seconds, then repeat part of what has been said or speak steadily for five seconds, hesitate, falter, then continue to speak steadily.
Voice Pitch	L—	Low. The conductor is speaking in lowest register.
	V—	Variable. Varying from high to low pitches so that it is impossible to categorize the entire interval as either high or low.
	H—	High. The conductor speaks in highest register.
Voice Volume	S—	Soft. Whispering. Barely audible.
	N—	Normal speaking voice.
	L—	Loud. Shouting above group or giving loud approvals, disapprovals, or instructions.
Mannerisms		Additional behaviors whose frequency of occurrence is so great that they are annoying or distracting.

Observation procedures for the Music Conductor Observation Form are identical to those described for the Choral and Instrumental Observation Forms. However, it is recommended that several observation sequences be used in completing the form. For example, during the first eight minutes of observation, the observer should look at only the first three categories on the form, activity, body movement, and conducting gestures; during the second eight-minute sequence, the observer should concentrate on two categories, eye contact and facial expression; during the third, the remaining categories of speech speed, voice pitch, and voice volume. Beginning observers may want to proceed through as many as five observational sequences in order to complete the form. The more experienced observer may be able to complete the form in two or three observational sequences.

This form is best used with videotaped rehearsals (see Appendices N and O) so that the same rehearsal segment can be analyzed in all categories. However, successful use of the form has been accomplished in live rehearsals. Here students are sensitized to each category of conductor behavior rather than to the *total* conducting behavior.

NOTES

[1]Albert Bandura, *Principles of Behavior Modification* (New York: Holt, Rinehart, and Winston, 1969). Albert Bandura and Richard H. Walters, *Social Learning and Personality Development* (New York: Holt, Rinehart and Winston, 1963). Albert Bandura, "Vicarious Process: A Case of No-Trial Learning," in *Advances in Experimental Social Psychology,* ed. L. Berkowitz (New York: Academic Press, 1965), 2, 1–55.

[2]Bandura, *Principles of Behavior Modification,* p. 120.

[3]Wallace A. Kennedy and Herman C. Willcutt, "Praise and Blame as Incentives," *Psychological Bulletin,* 62 (1964), 323–32. Edward M. Hanley, "Review of Research Involving Applied Behavior Analysis in the Classroom," *Review of Educational Research,* 40 (1970), 597–625. K. I. Altman and T. E. Linton, "Operant Conditioning in the Classroom Setting: A Review of the Research," *Journal of Educational Research,* 64 (1971), 277–86. Dewey Lipe and Steven M. Jung, "Manipulating Incentives to Enhance School Learning," *Review of Educational Research,* 41 (1971), 249–80.

[4]Wesley C. Becker and others, "The Contingent Use of Teacher Attention and Praise in Reducing Classroom Behavior Problems," *Journal of Special Education,* 1 (1967), 287–307. Charles H. Madsen, Jr. and others, "An Analysis of the Reinforcing Function of 'Sit-Down' Commands," in *Readings in Educational Psychology,* ed. Ronald K. Parker (Boston: Allyn and Bacon, 1968), pp. 265–78. R. Vance Hall, Diane Lund, and Deloris Jackson, "Effects of Teacher Attention on Study Behavior," *Journal of Applied Behavior Analysis,* 1 (1968), 1–12.

[5]Charles H. Madsen, Jr., Wesley C. Becker, and Don R. Thomas, "Rules, Praise and Ignoring: Elements of Elementary Classroom Control," *Journal of Applied Behavior Analysis,* 1 (1968), 139–50.

[6]Don R. Thomas, Wesley C. Becker, and Marianne Armstrong, "Production and Elimination of Disruptive Behavior by Systematically Varying Teacher's Behavior," *Journal of Applied Behavior Analysis,* 1 (1968), 35–45.

[7]David S. Holmes, "The Application of Learning Theory to the Treatment of a School Behavior Problem: A Case Study," *Psychology in the Schools,* 3 (1966), 355–59. Madsen, Jr. and others, "An Analysis of the Reinforcing Functions of 'Sit-Down' Commands."

[8]Portia Lee, "The Effect of Approval Mistakes of Reinforcement on Classroom Behavior" (unpublished Master's thesis, Florida State University, 1975).

[9]K. Daniel O'Leary and Wesley C. Becker, "The Effects of the Intensity of a Teacher's Reprimands on Children's Behavior," *Journal of School Psychology,* 7 (1968-69), 8-11. K. Daniel O'Leary and others, "The Effects of Loud and Soft Reprimands on the Behavior of Disruptive Students," *Exceptional Children,* 37 (1970), 145-55.

[10]Siegfried Englemann, "The Effectiveness of Direct Verbal Instruction on I.Q. Performance and Achievement in Reading and Arithmetic," in *An Empirical Basis for Change in Education,* ed. Wesley C. Becker (Chicago: Science Research Associates, 1971), p. 472.

[11]Charles H. Madsen, Jr. and Clifford K. Madsen, *Teaching/Discipline: A Positive Approach for Educational Development,* expanded 2nd ed. for professionals (Boston: Allyn and Bacon, 1974).

[12]Jere L. Forsythe, "The Effect of Teacher Approval, Disapproval, and Errors on Student Attentiveness: Music Versus Classroom Teachers," in *Research in Music Behavior,* eds. Clifford K. Madsen, R. Douglas Greer, and Charles H. Madsen, Jr. (New York: Teachers College Press, Columbia University, 1975), pp. 49-55. Terry Lee Kuhn, "The Effect of Teacher Approval/Disapproval on Attentiveness, Musical Achievement, and Attitude of Fifth-Grade Students," in *Research in Music Behavior,* eds. Clifford K. Madsen, R. Douglas Greer, and Charles H. Madsen, Jr. (New York: Teachers College Press, Columbia University, 1975), pp. 40-48.

[13]Robert L. Spradling, "The Use of Positive and Negative Reinforcement in a Rehearsal Situation" (unpublished paper, Florida State University, 1969). Kenneth Murray, "The Effect of Teacher Approval/Disapproval on Musical Performance, Attentiveness, and Attitude of High School Choruses," in *Research in Music Behavior,* eds. Clifford K. Madsen, R. Douglas Greer, and Charles H. Madsen, Jr. (New York: Teachers College Press, Columbia University, 1975), pp. 165-80.

[14]Cornelia Yarbrough, "The Effect of Magnitude of Conductor Behavior on Students in Selected Mixed Choruses," *Journal of Research in Music Education,* 23 (Summer 1975), 134-46.

[15]R. Douglas Greer and others, "Adult Approval and Students' Music Selection Behavior," *Journal of Research in Music Education,* 21 (Winter 1973), 345-54. Laura G. Dorow and R. Douglas Greer, "The Reinforcement Values of a Music Instrument for Beginning Instrumentalists and the Influence of Discovery versus Teacher Approval on Achievement," *Journal of Music Therapy,* XIV (Spring 1977), 2-16. Laura G. Dorow, "The Effect of Teacher Approval/Disapproval Ratios on Student Music Selection and Concert Attentiveness," *Journal of Research in Music Education,* 25 (Spring 1977), 32-40.

[16]Jere L. Forsythe, "Elementary Student Attending Behavior as a Function of Classroom Activities," *Journal of Research in Music Education,* 25 (Fall 1977), 228-39.

[17]Clifford K. Madsen, David E. Wolfe, and Charles H. Madsen, Jr., "The Effect of Reinforcement and Directional Scalar Methodology on Intonational Improvement," *Council for Research in Music Education,* no. 18 (1969), 22-23.

[18]R. Douglas Greer, Andrew Randall, and Craig Timberlake, "The Discriminate Use of Music Listening as a Contingency for Improvement in Vocal Pitch Acuity and Attending Behavior," *Council for Research in Music Education,* no. 26 (1971), 10-18.

[19] Murray, "The Effect of Teacher Approval/Disapproval." Yarbrough, "The Effect of Magnitude of Conductor Behavior."

[20] Yarbrough, "The Effect of Magnitude of Conductor Behavior."

[21] Material selected from *Teaching/Discipline* reprinted with permission from Allyn and Bacon, Boston, Massachusetts.

[22] Madsen and Madsen, *Teaching/Discipline,* pp. 234–35.

[23] Madsen and Madsen, *Teaching/Discipline,* pp. 240–41.

[24] Madsen and Madsen, *Teaching/Discipline,* p. 250.

[25] Madsen and Madsen, *Teaching/Discipline,* pp. 247–49.

[26] Madsen and Madsen, *Teaching/Discipline,* p. 237.

[27] Madsen and Madsen, *Teaching/Discipline,* pp. 242–54.

[28] Madsen and Madsen, *Teaching/Discipline,* pp. 177–94.

[29] Madsen and Madsen, *Teaching/Discipline,* pp. 244–46.

[30] Randall S. Moore, "The Effects of Videotaped Feedback and Self-Evaluation Forms on Teaching Skills, Musicianship and Creativity of Prospective Elementary Teachers," *Council for Research in Music Education,* 47 (Summer 1976), 1–7.

chapter 4

Designing and managing musical learning

Exercises in self-organization and time management, procedures for the solution of inappropriate social and academic music behaviors, techniques of establishing long-term and short-term goals, the attainment of habits of constant student and self-evaluation of lesson/rehearsal presentations. Field experiences include:

1. *Changing Your Behavior: Time Organization*
2. *Changing Student Behavior*
3. *Planning for Effective Music Instruction*
   a. *Classroom Music Teaching*
   b. *Instrumental and Vocal Lessons*
   c. *Rehearsals*
4. *Suggestions for Self-Evaluation*
5. *Setting Competencies for Yourself and Others*

Many successful music educators have attested to the fact that the process of designing effective learning sequences followed by the process of managing and evaluating those designs is the most difficult and time-consuming task in the profession of teaching. Effective designing or planning initially involves establishing long-term and short-term musical and social goals for you and your students.

Establishing goals requires both clarification and modification of your values as a music educator and professional musician. In addition, it requires consideration of parental, administrative, societal, and student value systems in determining the kinds of musical experiences you will provide. This first step also involves coming to grips with who, what, and why you will be teaching. As you struggle with these issues concerning value systems different from your own, you may find yourself choosing to compromise your own musical goals as a professional musician with your musical goals for students who are not professional musicians. Indeed, in this initial procedure you may decide that what you as a professional musician understand and value in music will not necessarily be shared by those students who will become consumers and/or amateur performers of music. Therefore, in the process of choosing music education values, you may decide to expand your goals to include not only the training of young artists but also the preparation of future consumers and amateurs.

After you have made the essential decisions regarding value issues, you must learn to envision the future such that you will be able to determine goals and design an effective learning sequence for a period of several years. For example, directors of performing organizations on the high school level may want to plan for a four-year time period since they are often responsible for the musical education of a student from the freshman through the senior years. Likewise, elementary music teachers may want to outline musical concepts and learning sequences for the years from kindergarten through the sixth grade. The advantages of this long-term planning include the higher probability that students as they progress from the first year through the final year will be exposed to a variety of literature, performing experiences, and will have a better understanding of such basic musical concepts as melody, rhythm, harmony, form, and so forth.

When you have clarified your values and outlined long-term goals for a projected period of time, you must consider other elements which might dictate the design of more detailed planning. For example, planning for a performing organization might entail considerations of: (1) appropriate literature for the concert season or topic and for teaching comprehensive musicianship; (2) appropriate literature for audience appeal; and (3) amount of rehearsal time available. Lesson planning for other courses such as music history or music theory might begin with a particular textbook. In this case, goals, objectives, unit plans, and daily lessons might be based on the materials suggested by the textbook.

As you break larger time periods down into smaller time periods, your planning should become more and more detailed so that by the time you get to the semester time period, for example, your planning might consist of not only a list of goals, but also objectives, specific assignments, a list of texts and materials, and a daily calendar. From this semester unit plan, you will want to break the time period down into days. As you do this, of course, your planning becomes even more specific. For each daily lesson or rehearsal there would be definite objectives, materials you plan to use, specified student and teacher responses, a list of audio-visual materials and equipment, concepts to be taught, and an evaluation section. Examples of daily lesson plans are found in *Contemporary Music Education*.[1] Although it is true that the ability to predict the rate of student progress is learned through experience, a case might also be made for the fact that student progress might occur at a faster pace if a plan had been created *a priori*, if records had been kept concerning the successes and failures of that plan, and if, finally, the plan had been revised based on feedback from students and other means of evaluation.

The ultimate goal is a sequence of musical experiences spanning the time period of several years which increases the probability that the very best musical education will occur for your students. Remember that your first attempt will be extremely difficult and time-consuming. It will seem easier just to "take one day at a time." However, the most effective and efficient learning sequence is one which has been (1) carefully and painstakingly thought through from beginning to end; (2) thoroughly tested without altering the original plan; (3) evaluated by students, yourself, and perhaps other teachers; and (4) revised according to these evaluations.

FIELD EXPERIENCES

1. Changing Your Behavior: Time Organization

Nearly all music students are able to remember teachers who seemed to be well-organized both inside and outside of rehearsal. It is easy for most students to recall past teachers who used rehearsal time efficiently as well as those who seemed to be always in the process of "getting themselves together." One of the problems with analyzing music situations is that often there is a disparity between thinking about the use of time and the actual processes for spending time wisely. Getting organized generally refers to both planning wisely and using your time effectively—all the time.

Because of a disparity between ideas and behavior, it is possible for you to think that you are doing one thing with your time when you are really doing something else. For example, most musicians know that they must spend a good deal of time practicing in order to develop increased musical skills. It would not do them much good to spend most of the time they intended for practice dreaming about how famous they will become when they are exceptional performers.

One of the most important aspects of developing effective techniques for teaching and living is to be honestly aware of how you spend your time. The most critical difference between a behavioral approach which pinpoints observable and measurable behaviors and less systematic approaches to human interactions is the keeping of behavioral records. Without records it is easy to pretend that things are happening when indeed they are not. It is also possible, if you know approximately how you are spending your time, to allow for some well-deserved leisure time in order to maintain a balance between "working" and "playing." While some aspects of music teaching and learning are so pleasant that it is not possible to tell which is work and which is play, often a few hours of change in activity is needed in order to be most effective.

After having completed the following exercises, most people are truly astounded to find how they actually spend their time. Sometimes all that is needed in order to change even major aspects of one's life is finally to realize how time is being spent. Often we find that the very things that we consider to be the least productive and most distasteful are consuming most of our time. After the following logs have been made, it will be possible to structure to a much greater extent the effective use of your personal and professional time.

a. Time Log A: Personal Time

First, keep a detailed record of what you do and when you do it, for 48 hours. For example:

Time Log: Tuesday, October 15

7:10	Awake
7:11	Bathroom, shower, dress
7:30	Breakfast
7:40	Gathered stuff, left for school
8:00	Arrived at school, went to teacher's lounge
8:30	Set up Concert Band
8:50	Talked to students
9:05	Concert Band
9:55	Clarinet class
11:00	Talked with teacher across the hall
11:30	Lunch
12:00	Lunch duty
12:30	Clarinet lesson
1:00	Teachers' lounge
1:15	Fire drill
1:20	Tightened drum head
1:30	Paper work
2:00	Cornet lesson
2:30	Theory class
3:15	Teachers' meeting
4:15	Left for home
4:35	Arrived at home, bathroom, changed clothes
4:50	Started supper, watched TV, read paper
5:50	Ate supper, washed dishes
6:30	Watched TV
7:00	Graded papers, studied scores
8:30	Talked to friend on phone
8:45	Watched TV
10:00	Ate a snack
10:15	Watched TV
11:00	Went to bed

The time log would then be continued for another 24-hour period. The more detailed the log is, the easier it will be for you to make significant changes for increased happiness. At the end of the 48-hour recording period, look critically at the time log and check the following.

(1) Things you don't like to do. Are they things necessary to reach long-term goals? Do you *have* to do them? Do you have a choice? Do you choose to do them because they are necessary in order to attain a long-term goal?

(2) Things you *do* like. Are you spending enough time doing these? How can you restructure your time so that you can spend more time doing happy things?

Evaluate the way you spend your time, using the above guidelines. How do you want to change your behavior? For example, in evaluating the above time log, you might want to

(1) Spend less time watching TV.
(2) Spend more time with friend.
(3) Use time spent in teachers' lounge to grade papers and study scores so that time after school can be spent with friend.

Using your evaluation of your time log, try to restructure your time for your own happiness. *Continue to keep a time log until you have successfully restructured your time.*

The above exercise is one in pinpointing, recording, consequating,[2] and evaluating your own behavior. It may be outlined as follows:

Pinpoint:	Restructuring time. Time log kept for 48 hours indicated not enough happy activities. Subject wanted to increase pleasant activities and decrease unpleasant ones.
Record:	A time log was kept for 48 hours detailing what time an activity began, what time it ended, and when a new activity began. Activities listed on the time log were then categorized, e.g., necessities (eating, sleeping, grooming, etc.); recreation; time spent with loved ones; time spent on schoolwork. A check was made of which activities were liked and not liked.
Consequate:	A careful evaluation of those activities not liked was attempted. It was decided that more time would be spent with friend and less time watching TV. Also, time previously spent in teachers' lounge would be used for grading papers and studying scores.
Evaluate:	A second 48-hour time log was kept. Results indicated that more time was spent with loved ones and in recreational activities; less time was spent sleeping, doing busy work, and talking to people the subject did not like. Also, time at home was spent with things other than schoolwork except for extra rehearsals.

Note: Although it took approximately three weeks of continuous recording to successfully restructure this teacher's time, he reported that the subsequent increase in happy activity was well
worth it.

b. Time Log B: Professional Time

In addition to restructuring your personal time, you may also want to
restructure the way you spend your professional time. Perhaps you are
wasting your time by doing things which could be done more efficiently
by others, or perhaps you are wasting students' time by allowing non-
learning activities to monopolize class time. You may be neglecting important things like communicating with colleagues and systematic observation of other teachers and students. Perhaps your students are not
responding to you because you have not spent enough time reading
about, writing, discussing, and practicing your lesson or rehearsal plans.

To check the way you spend your professional time, record the
number of hours you spend observing others, planning lessons, talking
with others during school hours, teaching others, changing behavior in a
systematic way, and participating in or supervising extracurricular activities. A Professional Time Log form has been designed to help you in
recording, analyzing, and modifying your professional time (see Appendix H).

A first-year teacher was encouraged to keep a professional time log
when she complained: "Nothing is going right. My classes are falling
apart. I can't seem to get myself together." Subsequent analysis of her
time log revealed that she was using her professional time as follows:

(1.) Observing (watching others teach and learn)	10%
(2.) Preparing for teaching (lesson planning)	25%
(3.) Talking with others (building professional and personal relationships with colleagues)	26%
(4.) Teaching	34%
(5.) Systematically changing inappropriate social and/or academic behavior	5%
(6.) Extracurricular duties	0%

She was quite surprised when she discovered that 26% of her time had
been spent talking to others. She frankly admitted that most of the time
she was seeking help for her problems rather than using the time to *do*
something constructive to solve them. In addition, she was concerned
that she had spent so little time in systematically changing inappropriate
behavior.

After a careful self-evaluation during which she thought about and listed her values concerning teaching, she decided to try to restructure her time by *decreasing* the time spent talking about her problems and increasing the time spent systematically changing students' inappropriate social and/or academic behavior. Eight weeks later she reported that "things" were "going much better." Her professional time log for the current week indicated a 15% decrease in time spent talking with others about her problems and a 15% increase in time spent systematically changing behavior. She reported that, although many of her teaching ideas had not been successful, she was happier when trying to do something about them than she was when she merely talked about her problems with others. In addition, she felt that she was learning how to deal with those problems more effectively and efficiently.

In structuring personal and professional time, you should first arrange your values concerning all aspects of your life—people, teaching, places, material things, ideas—in value hierarchies, listing them in order from most important to least important. Consider whether you must spend time doing unpleasant things in order to obtain a long-term value or goal. Then keep daily personal and professional time logs to determine how your time is spent. And, finally, restructure your time in order to get your behavior in line with your values.

2. Changing Student Behavior

Here are some examples of pinpoints successfully completed by university student teachers. It should be remembered that these pinpoints represent attempts by student teachers to change behavior in a systematic manner. They should be viewed only as examples by ordinary student teachers trying to deal with music problems within their intern situations. Further research will be necessary to validate the complete efficacy of these procedures. Nevertheless, they show how creative students can use behavioral techniques in an effective way. They are presented as example of a simple evaluation technique. The procedure is as follows:

a. *Pinpoint* (select by observation) an inappropriate academic or social behavior. Examples of inappropriate academic behavior might be playing incorrect rhythms, singing out of tune, playing or singing too loudly, and incorrect answers to verbal or written questions. Examples of inappropriate social behavior might be tearing the music, throwing drum mallets across the room, making unnecessary noise with instruments, talking during rehearsal, or any off-task behavior (see discussion under observation of individual students, Chapter Three).

b. After a behavior has been pinpointed, observe and *record* the number of times the behavior occurs during one hour, one day, or one week.

c. Now think of a way to change that behavior (*consequate*). Techniques are discussed and listed in Part II of *Teaching/Discipline*.[3] Initially attempt to use a potential reinforcer that is both positive and with which you feel comfortable before you resort to punishers.

d. After you have applied the consequence for several hours, days, or weeks, you should *evaluate* the effect of the technique you chose to change the inappropriate behavior (pinpoint). To evaluate, simply count and record the number of times the inappropriate behavior occurs during one hour, one day, or one week (whatever time period you chose for the initial recording). If the number of times the behavior occurs has not decreased, try again. Select another technique or go back to *consequate* in the modification sequence.

Examples of the Pinpoint, Record, Consequate, Evaluate Procedure

Number I: Second Grade Vocal Music

Pinpoint:	Child cried at the end of music class, and got attention of music teacher.
Record:	Child cried at the end of music class for two weeks (4 times).
Consequate:	When I started teaching the second graders in the third week, I praised Jenny during class when she was participating and happy. When she cried at the end of class, I ignored her.
Evaluate:	After two weeks of this treatment, she would not cry at the end of class when I was in the room, but if the music teacher was, she would cry.

Number II: Sixth Grade General Music

Pinpoint:	Students calling out to teacher for help and bothering her while she is helping other students. An independent study situation where students are to wait in line for teacher's help.
Record:	Students calling out across room and cutting in line bothering teacher while she is helping other students—16 occurrences in one hour.
Consequate:	Teacher ignored all students who called out or came for help out of turn. Recognition was given only to those students who waited in line for teacher's help.
Evaluate:	The first day I tried ignoring inappropriate behaviors and acknowledging correct behavior. There were eleven inappropriate behaviors. The second day there were only five occurrences.

Number III: High School Band Rehearsal

Pinpoint: Student continued playing the tuba after others in his lesson group had stopped. As a result teacher had to repeat instructions several times for his benefit.

Record: First lesson—student continued playing eight times out of thirteen stops given by conductor.

Second lesson—nine times out of fifteen stops.

Consequate: Teacher ignored the student and his playing after stops and gave instructions to the rest of the group regardless of his playing.

Evaluate: Student's playing decreased noticeably during consequate. During last lesson, student's playing after being cut off occurred only once during lesson.

Number IV: Second Grade Vocal Music

Pinpoint: Inability to match pitch.

Record: Only about 20% on pitch in singing songs. All classes, 2½ hour sessions for 2 weeks, a tape recorder was used to help judge.

Consequate: Teacher asked each student to sing first note of song alone, after teacher sings it. Other students asked to judge if child was on pitch or not. The teacher waited until students were on pitch and praised them individually. Then hand levels, teacher and students, were used during the singing to help determine the high and low points and movements of the melody.

Evaluate: Eighty percent rather than 20% were on pitch (approximately), almost all students were able to get first note matched, and all *tried*.

Number V: Third Grade Vocal Music

Pinpoint: ⌐ Too much talking (unable to work well and complete assignments) in the music room.

Record: Children's loud talking bothers others when independent work time is in progress—60% incomplete assignments.

Consequate: Let children evaluate and reward themselves in a points system for good student behavior. Children can award themselves points if they are working quietly when an occasional and unpredictable "beep" is sounded by a tape recorder. The children note their earned points in a weekly reward record booklet. Points accumulate and can be used to obtain special privileges such as extra free reading minutes, choosing favorite room duties, extra art supplies.

Evaluate: Results gratifying. Children seem to be capable of maintaining their own good behavior when given control of their own records. There was a small amount of talking. It was much quieter and didn't bother others. Cheating seldom occurred. If a child did take undeserved rewards, the action seemed to serve as a reminder to be more careful next time.

Number VI: Elementary Vocal Music

Pinpoint: At the end of each phrase, several individuals would say "hey" distracting from the song.

Record: Thirty-one "heys" said during a five-minute period of working on one song.

Consequate I: Class told they could sing favorite song at end of class if during the first twenty minutes of twenty-five minute class there were fewer than twenty "heys." Teacher ignored "heys" except to count them.

Evaluate I: During 20-minute period there were sixteen "heys." Class sang favorite song.

Consequate II: Class told they could sing favorite song at end of class if during twenty minutes there were fewer than ten "heys."

Evaluate II: During twenty-minute period only three "heys" were heard. Class sang favorite song.

Note: No mention of this at next class was made. There were no "heys."

Number VII: Fifth Grade Chorus

Pinpoint: Embarrassment.

Record: Fifth-grade chorus students were preparing for the Christmas program. Individual singing was required as a part of a musical play. Out of a possible forty students who might volunteer to sing, only three students did at the first rehearsal. Other students made comments such as "No way" . . . "I'm not going to sing alone" . . . "You've got to be kidding!"

Consequate: Teacher praised the three students for their singing and also for being first to volunteer. Teacher smiled approvingly to the students.

Evaluate: At each rehearsal thereafter the number of students volunteering to sing solo increased. By the 4th rehearsal, 80 to 85% of the students asked to be chosen to sing. The teacher praised the students verbally and through facial expression. The quality of singing also improved at each successive rehearsal.

Number VIII: Seventh Grade Flute Lesson

Pinpoint: Two students constantly banging or dropping flute. Seventh grade band lesson (flutes)—7 students.

Record: Twelve occurrences in a 35-minute lesson.

Consequate I: Every time this behavior occurred I gave the lecture on "If only instruments could cry."

Evaluate I: Next lesson only 7 occurrences. Still there was damage to the instruments.

Consequate II: Every time a student dropped or banged his or her flute I made them set it down carefully for ten minutes while other students continued with lesson. This was a ten-minute "Instrument Healing Time."

Evaluate II: By fourth lesson no dropping or banging of flutes.

Number IX: Sixth Grade Vocal Music

Pinpoint: Sixth-grade student went up to piano and played it after music class was over. (This was an inappropriate behavior because it disrupted the teacher's preparation time for the next class that was to come in.)

Record: Student did this every time for four classes in a row.

Consequate: Teacher told student that for every class he didn't play the piano he could come down once a week during his playtime and play the *electric* piano for ten minutes.

Evaluate: After his next music class he was awarded his first ten minutes to play the electric piano.

Number X: High School Voice Class

Pinpoint: Students constantly not coming to voice class. High school vocal program.

Record: During first week, 100 students out of 176 students did not come to voice class.

Consequate I:	Announced in large choir that voice classes are a necessity to learn music. List of absentees would be posted and it was their responsibility to make them up.
Evaluate I:	During second week, there was no improvement. In fact attendance decreased by about ten students.
Consequate II:	Different approach—posted sign saying, "The following students have *attended* voice class" and also indicated that everyone should try to get their names on the list.
Evaluate II:	At first, list was small, until students read the sign. Then attendance improved. Students wanted their names posted on the board. Over 100 students showed up for voice class.

Number XI: Second Grade Vocal Music

Pinpoint:	Laughing and clowning off-task behaviors.
Record:	Two boys off-task (laughing loudly, making faces, making noise) 75% of class time.
Consequate:	Boys were spoken to after class. Teacher explained that the class looked to them as leaders and that it was necessary for them to pay attention in class. We made a "secret pact" saying they would be my special helpers during the next class by behaving and thus setting an example for the rest of the class.
Evaluate:	Next class session boys were on-task 90% of the time with no distraction of class. They approached me after class to renew contract.

Number XII: Sixth Grade Vocal Music

Pinpoint:	Students calling out answers in class without raising hands.
Record:	Eleven times during one 30-minute class period.
Consequate:	During the next class I ignored the students' outbursts and called on those who raised their hands to answer. Also I praised those students who raised their hands.
Evaluate:	During the next thirty-minute class period, students' outbursts had been reduced to three times.

Number XIII: Junior High Band Rehearsal

Pinpoint:	Percussion section talking and acting silly between pieces in rehearsal when I conducted. On-task when master teacher conducted.

Record: First total rehearsal I conducted, there was unnecessary talking between every piece.

Consequate: Between rehearsals, I made friends with the percussionists. Told them how important they were and how I and the band depended upon them. Established rapport by being friendly in lesson, hall, lunch. Complimented them in band when they were on-task. If they were off-task, I ignored them and started pieces even if they were not ready.

Evaluate: Next rehearsal, percussion section slow getting ready only between second and third pieces. During the following rehearsal, students slow getting ready only before the first piece. No talking and acting silly between other pieces.

Note: Sometimes discipline problems can be solved by simply establishing a personal relationship with the student.

Number XIV: Middle School Chorus

Pinpoint: Failure to clean up room following music class papers, music on floor.

Record: Students have generally maintained a very clean room but recently the amount of scrap paper and extra music left on the risers has increased by 30%.

Consequate: Teacher reintroduced tidiness of the room as a serious part of the point system used every day. For every scrap of paper left on the floor students lost five points.

Evaluate: Students needed only one reminder (they lost 15 points) and the room returned to its original tidiness. Students were then praised for their behavior.

3. Planning for Effective Music Instruction

a. Classroom Music Teaching

The phrase "music in the classroom" refers to those most important teaching situations outside of the performance organization: the elementary music class; the general music class; the general music class in middle school or junior high school; the music history, theory, appreciation, or literature class; the humanities or related arts class; and others. In these teaching situations music is approached in a more comprehensive way through listening, composing, verbalizing, conceptualizing, and performing.

After you have completed the initial stages of planning as outlined in the general introduction to this field experience, you will be ready to make more specific and detailed lesson plans including behavioral objectives, time allotments, procedures (what you will do, how the student will respond, audio-visual aids), and evaluation procedures. The following chart (see figure 4-1) will help you begin to think systematically regarding learning situations. It contains suggestions for musical objectives, concepts, and skills, and provides a simple procedure for developing musical behavioral objectives.

You may want to use a cassette or reel-to-reel tape to evaluate daily lessons for the first three or four weeks or until you can master the skill of constantly monitoring both your own and students' behavior. Evaluation can also include written or oral tests, behavioral observation, attitude surveys, performance ratings, etc. The suggested Daily Lesson Plan (see figure 4-2) will help you to plan and record each day's progress efficiently (see Appendix E for blank form).

b. Instrumental and Vocal Lessons

In situations where a large number of students are involved, you may find that the use of progress charts is both easier and more efficient. Progress charts provide a record of student achievement in such areas as practice time, number of pages or exercises completed in method books, attendance at lessons, scales, arpeggios, vocalises, solos, and other assignments (see Appendix F). Space is also provided to help you keep track of methods books and solos both in progress and completed.

You can also use a progress chart to rate students' progress in sight-reading, rhythmic skills, knowledge of musical terms and concepts (see figure 4-1 for a complete list), technical ability (bowing, embouchure, slide positions, fingering, breath support, posture, articulation), solos, intonation, interpretation (expression, phrasing, style, tempo), tone quality, and diction. Other assignments or areas that you may want to check can also be added.

By using a rating system in conjunction with the progress chart, student attention is directed to more specified musical behaviors which you expect him/her to achieve. The method of rating which you use on a progress chart can be selected according to the grading system in your school, or you may decide to use a competitive point system. If you elect to use the point system, there are a variety of options open to you. First, you might pinpoint a specific problem area such as practice time and award points to students for increasing the amount of practicing they do. By keeping a practice progress chart posted in your rehearsal room, students can compare points they earn with those earned by others. This is often the only incentive needed to solve practice problems. This technique has also been successfully applied to a complete performing or-

Suggested Components of Behavioral Objectives in Music Education

Questions to be Answered in Writing Behavioral Objectives	Examples of Verbs Used in Writing Behavioral Objectives		Musical Concepts/Techniques/Instruments to be Mastered
	General Verbs	Musical Verbs	

Questions to be Answered in Writing Behavioral Objectives

Who?
- By whom?
- To Whom?
- With whom?

What?
- With what?
- To what?
- What will be heard?
- What will be observed?
- What will be produced?
- What will be judged?

How?
- In what way?
- Aurally? Visually?
- How many?
- How much?
- How little?
- How often?
- How well?
- How long?

Who will do what?
- How?
- Where?
- When?

General Verbs

verbalize, comment, express, relate, report, repeat, explain, react, decide, determine, select, review, research, distinguish, differentiate, group, isolate, match, outline, compare, combine, finalize, explore, research, consider, discover, question, discuss, investigate

Musical Verbs

General: crescendo, decrescendo, accelerate, retard, listen, conduct, accompany, rehearse, play, sing, phrase, improvise, perform, sight read, practice, write, tape, participate, involve, chord, present, teach, organize, identify, follow, interpret, imitate, compose, create, vary, alter, dictate, analyze, select, recreate, experiment, discriminate, recognize, orchestrate, score, notate, choreograph, dramatize, illustrate, arrange

Vocal: sing, chant, call, yell, hum, sigh, moan, whistle, shriek

Instrumental: shake, strike, pluck, rub, bow, scrape, strum, stroke, play, blow

Body Movement: leap, march, step, hop, dance, tiptoe, slide, roll, spin, circle, swing, bend, skip, sway, swoop, jump, somersault

Head: blink, nod, turn, shake, flop

Feet and Legs: tap toes, mark time, click heels, step high

Hands and Arms: tap, catch, snap, clap, shake, roll, point, throw, catch, give, reach, take, gather, conduct, cue

Musical Concepts/Techniques/Instruments to be Mastered

Melodic Concepts: contours, phrases, pitch, sequence

Melodic Instruments: bells, recorder, piano

Rhythm Concepts: beat, meter, patterns, duration

Rhythm Instrument: drum, tambourin, sticks

Harmonic Concepts: interval, chords, part singing

Harmonic Instrument: piano, guitar, autoharp

Form: types, cultural and historical orgins, listening, reading, composing

Other Concepts: tempo, mood, timbre, dynamics, tonalities, staff, clef, notation, lines & spaces, signs, symbols, key signatures

Figure 4-1

DAILY LESSON PLAN

when?

20 minutes

who?

Pinpoint: At the end of (class, lesson increment) the   class

will demonstrate acceptable   student

group

class

What?

singing and stepping
to quarter and eighth
notes

How?

singing and stepping the rhythm
of the song, "Sewing Needle"
with 95% accuracy while stand-
ing next to desks with eyes closed

by _____

Examples:
Performance ability
sight-singing proficiency
research of the classical
    period

Examples:
Playing the entire piece with-
    out stopping
Sight-reading 8 measures with
    80% accuracy
Submitting a 20-page report
    free from factual error

Record: (See above format)

At the beginning of the   lesson   the
_____ class _____ demonstrated _____ approximately
20% accuracy in stepping quarter and eighth-note rhythm
combinations
by stepping the rhythm to the song, "Sewing Needle" at their
desks with their eyes closed.

Consequate: *Time allotted for lesson or lesson increment:*   20 minutes

A. What you will do: Teach song - extrapolate combinations of   and   notes; have students imitate with steps, claps and words - play game with
students in a chain, "sewing" each other - allow
students to lead the needle while singing and
stepping

B. How the student will respond
(anticipation of successes and failures):
Students will forget to step in rhythm in their
enthusiasm for the game - will need to prompt
for the first two or three leaders

C. Audio-visual aids (use at least two per lesson):
(1) small & large pictures of needles & thread
corresponding to rhythm of song
(2) Metallophone to play ostinato

Evaluate: A. Students' successes and failures: approximately
30% of students were not able to transfer the idea
of stepping in the game to stepping in place

B. Teacher's successes and failures: Failed to teach for
transfer from game to stepping in place - successful
in teaching song and eliciting imitation from
students

Figure 4-2 Daily Lesson Plan Example

ganization including improvisation, playing a second instrument, conducting the group and so on.[4]

To help you and the student keep an accurate record of practice time, you may require a weekly practice report. This practice report would contain the student's name, the number of hours and minutes practiced per day for one week, and the parent's signature for verification.

c. Rehearsals

After you have (1) decided your strategy for the largest time period (perhaps four or more years); (2) broken that time period down into smaller segments; and (3) systematically designed a musical learning sequence for those smaller segments, you will be ready to plan the daily rehearsal.

The following chart (see figure 4-3) contains some suggested components of ensemble rehearsals. The chart is divided into columns which represent the various segments of the ensemble rehearsal time period. The first column includes various musical concepts which can be effectively taught during the warm-up time period. The second column contains a brief sightreading task analysis. Finally, the next four columns represent various musical and extramusical concepts and techniques which can be taught through carefully selected musical literature. This chart is not intended to be all-inclusive. It is intended to be a stimulus for more creative and productive rehearsal planning.

Effective rehearsals should always include brief warm-up exercises, practice in sightreading, and rehearsal of the concert repertory. The suggested Daily Rehearsal Plan (see figures 4-4, 4-5 and Appendix G) does not substitute for marking your score. On the contrary, it can be a valuable addition to your planning for optimal use of rehearsal time.

On the form, space is provided for you to jot down notes concerning concepts and techniques you want to teach through the rehearsal of each composition. At the bottom of the form there is space for an evaluation of the rehearsal. Here you can list problems encountered and suggest possible solutions which you can try at the next rehearsal.

To evaluate further the effectiveness of the rehearsal you may wish to tape it and listen critically for deviations from your original plan as well as for student performance problems.

4. Suggestions for Self-Evaluation

Evaluation of teaching will be done periodically by an administrator in the school. These evaluations might consist of input from several different sources. First, an administrator might observe teaching/learning in the classroom. This observation might be preceded by a conference in which the principal discusses the lesson plan for the day of the

SUGGESTED COMPONENTS OF ENSEMBLE REHEARSALS

WARM – UPS	SIGHTREADING	COMMON MUSICAL CONCEPTS/TECHNIQUES	MUSICAL CONCEPTS/TECHNIQUES		EXTRA – MUSICAL CONCEPTS
			INSTRUMENTAL	VOCAL	
Intonation	Melodic Concepts: pitch, scales, modes, sustained tones, intervals, chromaticism, etc.	Performance style, blend, attacks/releases, dynamics, balance, intonation, tempo timbre, posture, conducting, breath support	Performance accompanying Technical Problems: bowing, fingering, embouchure, tonguing, slide positions, special effects, embellishments, ranges, techniques, articulation trill fingerings, alternate fingerings, overtone series, holding and hand position	Performance Diction: English, French, German, Italian, Russian, Latin Technical Problems: range, tessitura, voice break, falsetto, chest voice, glottal attacks, aspirate "H", resonance, cambiata A Capella singing Memorization	Performance Etiquette Care of Voice/Instrument Equipment: stands, chairs, piano, stroboscope, instruments, sound equipment, risers Supplies: reeds, valve and slide oil, pegs, strings, percussion equipment
Balance					
Blend					
Breathing		Analysis form and texture critical listening score reading harmonic, melodic, rhythmic			Seating Arrangements
Phrasing					
Technical Problems	Rhythmic Concepts: beat, meter, duration, accent	Composition notation, arranging improvising	Analysis Instrumental Forms concerto, suite symphony, tone poem, scherzo, rondo, fugue, sonata, allegro, march, variation, overture, ballet, toccata, minuet, rhapsody	Analysis Vocal Forms: opera, cantata, oratorio, madrigal, motet, requiem, canon, musical comedy, balletta operetta, magnificat, mass text	Concert Organization: posters, newspaper articles, stage set-up, programs, uniforms TV and Radio Production
Rhythmic Problems	Dynamic Concepts: loud, soft, crescendo, decrescendo, diminuendo, etc.				
Warm-up Instrument and Voice		Listening ear training recognition of period, style, form, texture, tonality, timbre, harmony, melody, rhythm, etc.			
Development of Positive Rehearsal Attitude	Technical Problems Notation (Rhythmic and Melodic)	Verbalization	Composition Instrumentation Orchestration Instrumental accompaniment	Composition Voice classification, range, tessitura Part-writing Arranging instrumental accompaniments	Stage Production: producing, directing, acting, stage design, lighting, make-up
	Recognition of melodic and rhythmic patterns form	Melodic Concepts: contour, phrase, sequence, etc.			Relating Music to other Artistic Disciplines
	Transposition	Rhythmic Concepts: patterns, syncopation, etc.			Historical, Cultural, Social Aspects
	Textural differences	Harmonic Concepts: interval, chord, major minor, modal, cadence, modulation, etc. Stylistic Concepts: staccato, legato, marcato, Renaissance Baroque, Classical, etc.			Biographical Material on Composers

Figure 4-3

DAILY REHEARSAL PLAN

Pinpoint:

1. To develop legato singing lines in each voice part.
2. To learn notes/rhythms of new piece. Rehearsal time: 55 minutes.

Record:

Warm-ups: Legato singing: 1. Breath control (#1, #2, #3)
                                     2. Resonance (#12, #13, #14)

Time: 5 minutes

Sightreading: "Wondrous Cool, Thou Woodland Quiet" (Brahms)
                 (new piece to be introduced)

Tape-Record This Reading

Review of Last Rehearsal: Have chorus sing through "Sure on This Shining Night" without stopping; mark score where problems occur

Tape-Record This Review

Consequate:

1. Work on notes/rhythms "Wondrous Cool"; work on legato style—15 minutes; TAPE-RECORD.
2. Explain legato singing style—demonstrate; play recordings of professional groups singing both pieces we are rehearsing and point out legato singing style—10 minutes.
3. Work on legato singing style in "Sure on This Shining Night"—15 minutes; TAPE-RECORD.

Evaluate:

Listened to Tape Recordings. Results:

1. Sightreading much improved: rhythms averaged 85% correct, notes 80% correct; sopranos still the weakest section; all sections need more chromatic work.
2. Legato style singing is improving; still some fading of sound on long notes; continue work on this tomorrow; new sightreading piece "Adoramus Te."
3. "Wondrous Cool"—work on notes & rhythms still needed (see data from sightreading)—especially sopranos and basses.
4. "Sure on This Shining Night"—intonation poor; continue to work on legato style singing; sensitize the group to intonation problems; sing passages which are poorest in tune in higher and lower keys; include intonation exercises in warm-ups.

Figure 4-4. Daily Rehearsal Plan example: Choral

DAILY REHEARSAL PLAN

Pinpoint:

To increase the awareness and accuracy of intonation in one prepared piece and transfer those concepts to a new piece during sightreading. Rehearsal time: 55 min.

Record:

1. Warm-up—10 minutes
   a. Exercise #29—for physical and mental warmup and establish rehearsal discipline.
   b. Exercise #42—for balance and intonation; increase "on-task" behavior.
   c. A♭ major scale in whole notes, ♩ = 60—to refine the ensemble pitch center; identify and correct major individual pitch discrepancies.
2. Review last rehearsal—5 minutes
   a. Play through 2nd mvt. of Holst Second Suite for Military Band in F without stopping. Tape-record.

Consequate:

1. Isolate intonational problems in the first four measures of Holst. Build F minor chord from the bottom and tune each chord member. Watch out for the concert A♭ in the alto sax and alto clarinet. Double check with a visual tuning device.
2. Proceed through the movement, stopping where necessary to:
   a. identify intonation problems.
   b. have student identify whether he/she is sharp or flat and then match the correct pitch aurally.
      Confirm correct pitches with visual tuning device.
      Time: 20 minutes.
3. Play through entire movement a final time and tape-record. Time 5 minutes.
4. Discuss briefly and identify potential intonation problems in Grainger's Irish Tune from County Derry. Sightread and tape-record. Time: 15 minutes

Evaluate:

1. Listened to first recording of Holst piece marking in the score where intonation problems occurred and noting who was having each problem.

2. Listened to the second recording of Holst piece, making note of which intonation problems were or were not corrected as well as who was having each problem. Much improvement, particularly in accompanying woodwind parts. Oboe and trumpet soloists still having trouble two measures after A.

3. Listened to Grainger piece, marking the score where intonation problems occurred. Paid particular attention to those places discussed with the band prior to sightreading. Many of these "problem spots" were quite good. The transfer of "intonational awareness" from Holst to Grainger was probably greatly aided by the anticipatory discussion prior to sightreading.

Figure 4-5 Daily Rehearsal Plan Example: Instrumental

observation. During the observation the principal might make notes concerning the appropriateness of the lesson, the general class atmosphere, methodology, class discipline, student participation, and the overall effectiveness of teacher communication. Following the observation, there might be a postobservation conference during which the administrator discusses strengths and weaknesses based on the observation.

In addition to regular observation by the administrative staff, some school systems require an annual self-evaluation report. In the annual report the teacher may be asked to define what has been taught during the past year, or to list courses, achievements, and/or performances. The teacher might also be asked to project activities for the coming year.

Other indicators of success for administrators may include a rising enrollment, an increase in the number of students participating in all-state organizations, awards and other recognition given to both individual students and performance groups, the number of performances given by students in and out of school, and the amount of community support the music program has.

Although administrative evaluations are often a protection in matters of tenure and professional rights, and although they give the teacher an idea of how the administrator feels about him/her both personally and professionally, they sometimes do not help improve the specific behavior of teaching music in the most efficient way. However, the input of colleagues who are nonmusicians is important if one is to have balance in professional life. Indeed it is a very necessary segment of the total evaluation component. It is vital to survival in the school as a complete entity.

In addition to evaluation by the administration of the school, other professional music educators may evaluate both teaching and student performance. The most common method of evaluation by other professional musicians is the festival or contest. However, there is an alternative which is not as widespread; that is, the use of professional absence days to observe and evaluate other music education programs. These observations can serve two purposes: (1) the observer can serve as an evaluator for the music teacher being observed; and (2) the observer can, through observation, learn new creative approaches to teaching music. In this way both the observer and the person being observed grow professionally through the process of evaluation.

Of course, evaluation of teaching and student progress can take place independently of other professional colleagues. Self-evaluation can involve using input about what the student has learned. That input can be in the form of tests or written papers, recordings of performances or rehearsals, or simply tape recordings of teaching/learning presentations from day to day. It can be videotapes of rehearsals, private lessons, or class situations. Attitude scales can be administered to students to determine likes and dislikes about the rehearsal, conductor, and the music. Finally, self-evaluation involves analyzing all the various inputs of professional colleagues critically. Good teaching is a process of constant self-reassessment, self-restructuring of goals, and self-improvement.

Evaluation can take place in various settings. For example, in the previous field experiences an evaluation component is always present. In the section concerning the study of the school system, organization, and services, there are a series of exercises and questions designed to acquaint the inexperienced teacher with various evaluation and measurement techniques used by school districts. In the section on developing resource materials, constant evaluation of materials is stressed as a card file is developed and interviews with other professional colleagues are conducted. Throughout this field experience the recommended technique for planning daily lessons and rehearsals emphasizes immediate evaluation of those lessons and rehearsals.

Having participated in the previous field experiences primarily as an evaluator of others, you should now transfer those techniques of observation and evaluation to the evaluation of yourself. The following outline will assist you in conducting a self-evaluation:

a. *Audiotape Recording*

Make a cassette or reel-to-reel tape recording of your class or rehearsal.

(1) Data to record
   (a) Number of approvals and disapprovals.
   (b) Number of minutes used for teacher instruction, performance or activity by the entire class, sectional rehearsal or small group activity, individual interaction.

    (c) Ratings of the performance of your group by other musicians (see Appendix I).

    (d) Ratings of your teaching by other teachers (see Appendices J, P, and Q).

(2) Using the data

    (a) Are you too negative? Research indicates that an 80% positive to 20% negative ratio is effective reinforcement.

    (b) Do you talk too much? Do you neglect individuals or certain sections? How did you plan to use class or rehearsal time? Did you follow that plan? If not, why?

    (c) Where were the lowest ratings on the performance of your group? Listen to the tape again. Why were these ratings low? How can you help the group improve?

    (d) How can you use the suggestions concerning your musicianship and teaching in your next lesson or rehearsal?

b. Videotape Recording

Make a videotape of yourself or your students in rehearsal, class, or individual lesson (see Appendix N).

(1) Data to record

    (a) Teacher Observation Form A (see Chapter Three, figures 3-3 and 3-4).

    (b) Music Conductor Observation Form (see Chapter Three, figures 3-8 and 3-9).

    (c) Choral/Instrumental Rehearsal Observation Forms (see Chapter Three, figures 3-6 and 3-7).

    (d) Elementary Music Teaching Evaluation Form (see Chapter Three, figure 3-5).

    (e) Student Observation Form C (see Chapter Three, figure 3-1).

(2) Using the data

    (a) Are you using a ratio of 80% approval to 20% disapproval? Are you making mistakes of reinforcement? How can you eliminate these errors? Are you giving approval for *socially* as well as academically appropriate behavior?

    (b) Are you singing along with the group too much? Do you talk too much? Are you annoying the group by moving around too much? Do you have enough expressive gestures in your conducting, or is it too expressive? Are you maintaining eye contact with the group, or are your eyes glued to the music? Do you smile enough? Is your speech variable enough to maintain student attention when they are not performing? (See Appendix O.)

    (c) How do you use rehearsal time? How much time is spent in sectional rehearsals, entire group rehearsal, instruction? Is the group more than 20% off-task?

(d) Did you indicate clearly to the class what musical concept you wanted them to learn? Was your presentation of that concept accurate? Was your lesson well-organized? Were you as creative as possible? How could you be more creative? How could you stimulate more creativity in your students?

c. Personal and/or Professional Time Log

(1) Data to record (see pages 72–75)
(2) Using the data (see pages 72–75)

d. Specifying Student Behavior

(1) Data to record (see pages 75–85)
(2) Using the data
   (a) How are you most effective in your interaction with students?
   (b) Are you skillful in handling discipline problems?

e. Measuring Achievement

Make a cassette or reel-to-reel tape of your performance group at the beginning and end of the semester or year. Also, give a written music achievement test at the beginning and end of the semester or year.

(1) Data to record
   (a) Ratings by outside judges on intonation, blend, balance, tempo, dynamics, etc.
   (b) Number of correct responses on achievement tests.
(2) Using the data
   (a) Compare pre- and postperformance ratings in each category on the performance rating form.
   (b) Compare pre- and posttest achievement test scores.

f. Attitude Surveys

Give attitude surveys at the beginning and end of the semester or year.

(1) Data to record
   (a) Attitude Survey for Performance Groups (see Appendix K).
   (b) Attitude Survey for Primary Grades (see Appendix L).
   (c) Attitude Survey for Upper Elementary Grades (see Appendix M).
   (d) Evaluation of Music Instruction (see Appendix Q).
(2) Using the data
   (a) Has student attitude improved since the beginning of the semester or year? Why or why not?

(b) What can you do to increase student enjoyment of music?

(c) How does student attitude compare with student performance? Do good performers have good attitudes? Do high achievers have good attitudes?

(d) Compare student attitude with student off-task as measured on the observation forms. Are students who have bad attitudes off-task?

g. Observations by Nonmusician Colleagues

Ask nonmusician administrators or other nonmusician faculty colleagues to observe you formally in your classroom or rehearsal.

(1) Data to record (See Appendix P)
  (a) Ratings of personal characteristics.
  (b) Ratings of communications skills.
  (c) Ratings of general and musical teaching ability.
  (d) Ratings of professional attitudes.
(2) Using the data
  (a) How do nonmusician colleagues view you as a teacher?
  (b) What can I do to improve in those categories with low ratings?

In summary, competency-based music education is a process in which the teacher is participating in a continuing cycle of (1) pinpointing specific objectives (2) recording, that is, analyzing the learning situation by taking data, (3) consequating, designing a specific plan for teaching/ learning, (4) evaluating the teaching and learning process and product, and (5) reanalyzing the learning situation by repeating the cycle. The experimenting teacher who provided the model for the foregoing field experiences in pinpointing, recording, consequating, and evaluating a learning sequence would continue to refine and test each step of the process using the latest developments in research and technology. It is a process emphasizing evaluation, systematic record-keeping, analysis, and the modification of the teaching/learning sequence based on analysis of the data.

NOTES

[1]Clifford K. Madsen and Terry Lee Kuhn, *Contemporary Music Education* (Arlington Heights, Ill.: AHM Publishing Corp., 1978).

[2]*Consequate* is a word you will not find in Webster's dictionary. It refers to the teaching strategy (use of approval/disapproval reinforcers) or the plan for dealing with a specified behavior (pinpoint).

³Charles H. Madsen, Jr. and Clifford K. Madsen, *Teaching/Discipline: A Positive Approach for Educational Development,* expanded 2nd ed. for professionals (Boston: Allyn and Bacon, 1974), pp. 59–172.

⁴William Zurcher, "A Data Based Credit System for Performing Groups," a paper read at the National Symposium-Research in Music Behavior, Atlanta, Georgia, in November, 1978.

chapter 5

The experimenting teacher

A summary of procedures outlined in chapters one through four and an application of competency-based characteristics to a course of study in basic conducting. Field experiences for this chapter involve using models for pinpointing, recording, consequating, and evaluating a course of study to design your own competency-based course or instructional sequence. Field experiences include:

1. *Pinpoint (Task Analysis)*
2. *Record (Pretest)*
3. *Consequate (Teaching Technique)*
4. *Evaluate (Process and Product)*

What is competency-based music education? The first aspect concerns a product or competency. In competency-based music education this means the ability *to do* something at a specified level of excellence. Traditionally, music educators have emphasized the cognitive objective: the ability to demonstrate knowledge or understanding concerning music education. The word "competency" however designates a shift in the focus and thrust of teacher education from cognitive to performance and consequence objectives. The music educator must not only "know about" teaching but must also be able to perform as a teacher and produce change (learning) in students. Learning defined as a product would include all measurable change regarding cognitive, performance, attitudinal, and experiential objectives.

Competency-based music education also concerns process. This process is a continuing cycle of analysis of the learning situation by taking data, designing a specific plan for teaching, evaluating the teaching and learning product, and reanalyzing the learning situation by again taking data. The teacher within a competency-based music education program may be characterized as an experimenting teacher. This teacher is involved in the process of competency-based music education: keeping records, specifying the learning task, systematic teaching, and evaluation of both the product and the process.

The role of the traditional teacher was to function as a source of knowledge or a presenter of information. In contrast, the experimenting teacher functions primarily as an evaluator, designer, and manager of the product and process of teaching and learning. The experimenting teacher as evaluator will find it difficult if not impossible to separate the evaluation of teacher performance from the evaluation of student performance, attentiveness, and attitude. This is due to the fact that the experimenting teacher is always learning (changing) as a result of the student's product and learning process, and the student within a competency-based music education program is always teaching the experimental teacher through interaction with the design and evaluation of both the process and product of the learning sequence.

The professional music educator as an experimenting teacher is responsible not only for having knowledge of the subject area to be taught (music) but also for having the skill to impart that knowledge to others. The skills of teaching valued by the authors of this book have been incorporated into carefully designed field experiences. They include: (1) a series of orientation exercises introducing the new teacher to school value systems; (2) experiences in the development of techniques of establishing long-term and short-term goals; (3) the development of constant and detailed record-keeping habits through a structured method of collecting materials and information concerning the teaching/learning of music; and (4) the development of a positive approach to teaching/conducting music through systematic observation, and again, record-keeping and analysis.

In this chapter as in the previous ones, the importance of record-keeping, constant evaluation, and change in keeping with the results of the evaluation is again emphasized. The method of evaluation suggested here is criterion-referenced rather than norm-referenced. The teacher/student is not evaluated in comparison with the performance of a larger group or test population. Rather the teacher/student is evaluated on the basis of his/her achievement of stated objectives and specified criteria (competency levels). A concept critical to this means of evaluation is self-evaluation. Ideally, in a competency-based program, the objectives, criteria, competency levels, and learning sequences are defined so clearly and specifically that students/teachers can assess for themselves whether or not objectives are being met.

In keeping with the criterion-referenced concept of evaluation, the authors believe that evaluation should ideally be initiated by the person being evaluated. Evaluation should be something that the individual who wishes to grow professionally would welcome. A useful evaluation initially requires a determination of one's past behavior as a teacher including both successes and failures. It might consist of objectively listing everything accomplished during the year and deciding whether one's actual behavior as a teacher matches one's idea or value concerning teaching. If at the end of this exercise in matching behavior with ideas or values, one considers oneself an ideal teacher, there would seem to be nothing to be concerned about, that is assuming administrative superiors agree with that assessment. Few of us are in this enviable position. Indeed, perhaps those who consider themselves "ideal" should take a few moments to reexamine themselves for reliability of judgment.

The ability to get "outside ourselves" for an objective look is difficult to develop. The act of learning about ourselves must involve input from other people. To ensure that evaluation will be meaningful, the teacher must take the initiative in deciding teaching values and in determining significant questions concerning music teaching and learning. Others whose opinions are valued can observe and evaluate teaching and learning, but their opinions will be meaningless if important issues concerning how one will teach, what will be taught, when new concepts will be introduced, why various kinds of music will be chosen, and who will be taught (consumers of music, young artists, or both) have not been decided.

A competency-based approach to teaching involves the application of certain characteristics. Included in those characteristics are (1) precise learning objectives defined in assessable behavioral terms; (2) individualized and self-paced course of study; (3) criterion-referenced rather than norm-referenced evaluation; and (4) a shift in emphasis from the teacher and the teaching process to the learner and the learning process.[1] It would appear that in the development of competency-based teacher education in music, extensive experimental, descriptive, and behavioral research is necessary. Throughout this process of research, techniques for teaching and learning must be scrutinized in a systematic way.

A useful technique for the study of teaching and learning is one developed through behavioral research in teaching.[2] This technique involves first pinpointing or specifying the exact behavior or task to be taught or learned. The pinpointed task must be examined thoroughly and defined precisely in terms of what the learner must actively "do" to perform the task successfully.

Second, data should be collected concerning the ability of the learner to perform the task before teaching begins. This involves recording the frequency of occurrence of the correct behavior(s) subsumed within the desired task. This technique may be called a *pretest*. The initial recording or pretest period is followed by a *consequate* applied to the pinpointed behavior.

The consequate is the teaching process itself. In competency-based teacher education, a teaching process (consequate) might involve a variety of technological tools, such as videotape, which ensure independence, individualization, and self-pacing. It would also involve constant recording, or record-keeping, by the student and teacher so that progress may be made at the most efficient rate. Finally, the entire procedure (pinpoint, record, consequate, or task analysis, pretest, teaching) is *evaluated* (posttest). In competency-based education evaluation helps the teacher to further pinpoint, specify, and analyze the original task. Thus, the procedure of pinpointing (task analysis), recording (pretest), consequating (teaching and learning through constant record-keeping), and evaluating (posttest) is a continuing cycle.

FIELD EXPERIENCES

The following section represents an *elaborated* example of competency-based instruction. It deals with the development of conducting skills. Developing conducting skills seems to be important in the preparation of all music teachers. Since virtually all university music programs include experiences in conducting, it was determined that the following model would provide a useful example of competency-based instruction.

The *Pinpoint* or task analysis of any complex set of skills (conducting) must include a good deal of specificity. The following example includes categories covering baton technique, beat patterns, preparations, releases, changes in tempo, dynamics, style, cueing, and eye contact. Each of these classifications is additionally broken down into other separate behaviors. It can be seen that a highly specific task analysis must be done before any complex activity can be efficiently learned.

The *Record* aspect of the following model includes data taken from music education majors as they attempted to master basic conducting skills. The above categories were observed and the percentage of each person's ability to do each specific behavior was determined.

Consequate experiences took the form of practicums where students practiced each skill with videotaped feedback. The *Evaluate* segment was essentially the same as the initial *Record* with improvement being determined by the gain in conducting skills across each category.

It is extremely advisable while proceeding through this model to keep in mind several important things. First, the model is intended as an *example* of competency-based instructional procedures. It is not intended as the definitive model for developing conducting skills. It must be remembered that there are many ways that the *art* of conducting could be analyzed and subsequently taught. Other approaches to teaching conducting could be entirely different from the following model. Indeed, it is a basic characteristic of competency-based instruction that the content and sequencing be determined by the values of the instructor and the students to be taught. The particular model presented here exemplifies one way in which conducting skills could be analyzed and developed within a practical teaching situation utilizing a competency-based approach. Perhaps after studying the following model, other approaches and specific skills could be developed that would be much better. Regardless, the necessity for devising behavioral objectives which can be observed and evaluated constitutes an important and formidable task.

Finally, the following model could be transferred to a variety of music teaching situations other than conducting. It would seem useful to use the model to thoroughly analyze and design learning experiences for general music (see figure 4-2) and choral/instrumental rehearsals (see figures 4-4 and 4-5). A useful beginning for any *Pinpoint* or task analysis might be a careful review of Chapter Two and Chapter Four with specific reference to figures 4-1 and 4-3. These chapters are also useful in developing appropriate *Consequates*. Chapters Three and Four will prove valuable when developing an *Evaluate* procedure.

> **Caution:** *The following pages are intended to demonstrate an application of a competency-based approach to a common aspect of teacher preparation experienced by most musicians (conducting). Because of the need for great specificity within a competency-based approach, this example may seem very long and involved. Remember that the following is not intended as a mini-conducting text. Please keep in mind that the purpose of this section is the analysis of beginning conducting skills. Do not get "lost" or "caught up" in the subject matter, rather view the following as one example concerning how a seemingly difficult and complex task such as conducting can be broken up in separate parts and subsequently analyzed.*

1. Pinpoint (Task Analysis)

The first step for the experimenting teacher is to pinpoint the task: what you want a person to be able to do at the end of a learning experience. For example, suppose you choose to teach a person to be able to conduct. You have decided that good conducting is modeling an affective response to music for the performing group and/or the audience. To further specify what is involved in modeling an affective response, i.e., conducting, one might observe videotapes of various conductors, read all conducting textbooks, and study various research reports.

Having done a thorough job of gathering all possible information concerning the task of conducting, one then might try to specify the skills involved in performing the task of conducting. One might conclude that conducting involves the skills of baton technique, left-hand technique, various nonverbal behaviors such as eye contact, body movement, facial expressions, various verbal skills such as demonstration, imagery, and musical or cognitive skills such as score reading and error detection. Having analyzed the entire task of conducting, one may further continue the task analysis in a more detailed and specified manner.

Thus, baton and left-hand technique become eight categories for technical skill development: beat pattern, tempo, dynamics, style, cueing, eye contact, preparations, releases. Each of these eight categories under the general heading, technique, would then be further broken down into operational definitions. The operational definitions would be clear, precise, and would contain illustrations where appropriate. The following are examples of operational definitions for the above eight skill categories (other operational definitions appear in Chapter Three as observational categories):

Beat Patterns: General Information

Location of the Beat

"In learning to conduct, the student should learn to place the various beats of each measure with care to avoid their wandering in a way which is difficult for the performers to follow."[3] Imagine a horizontal line at about chest height which is intersected by a vertical line about three inches to the right of the center of the conductor's body and relate the beats to this formation.

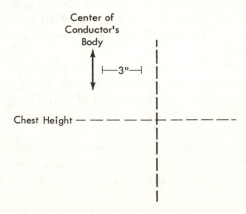

Left-Handed Conducting

The right hand is used primarily in beating time in conducting. Beginning conductors should all hold the baton with the right hand. Left-handed people (and a few right-handed) may at first experience some difficulty in leaving the left hand relaxed and using only the right hand. Most authorities agree that right-handedness in conducting is necessary, otherwise confusion may result in experienced performers.[4]

An effort should be made at the beginning stages to avoid using the left hand to mirror conduct—simultaneously conducting the beat pattern in mirror image with both hands. It is important that independence of hand movement be developed as early as possible. The use of the left hand will be described below.

The Baton

"The baton is the conductor's technical instrument...[and] has emerged (especially for the instrumental ensembles) as the most efficient means of conveying a precise message to the players..."[5] The technique of conducting with a baton should be mastered by all students.

The beat exists in a concentrated, easy to observe location—the point of the baton. The baton serves as an extension of the arm, putting the point of the beat out from the conductor's body in an area more easily seen by the players. A baton can prove to be a most efficient tool in providing clarity and expressiveness.

The stick (baton) is generally held between the tip of the thumb and the side of the index finger somewhere between the middle joint of the finger and the nail. The butt of the baton rests in the palm of the hand.[6]

The grip should be firm but relaxed, that is, the conductor must exercise control of the baton and yet feel at ease in holding it. An overly firm grip causes inflexibility in the wrist. Also, the position of the baton should be considered. It should not point upward from the hand or too far to the left. Rather, the stick should point outward from the body and slightly to the left.[7]

Batons are available in various lengths and weights. The choice of one should be based on comfort and applications. The sticks come with or without handles made of varying materials, usually wood or cork. A lightweight fiberglass baton with a cork handle seems to be generally accepted for beginners' use.

The ultimate decision of whether or not to use a baton must be made by the conductor based upon particular circumstances. However, the decision should take place only after much experience in conducting with the stick.

Posture

Each student should stand erect, with elbows relaxed, forearms slightly raised, baton extending away from the body at approximately chest height, and feet slightly parted with the right foot a bit more forward than the left for balance. This posture plus eye contact is imperative for starting the performing ensemble accurately.

The Two-Beat Pattern

The basic pattern for two beats per measure[8] is given in figure 5-1. Shown is a downward motion on the first beat, followed by an upward

Figure 5-1 Basic Pattern: Two Beats per Measure

motion on the second beat. The two-beat pattern typically appears as in figure 5-2 where the first beat occurs below the left-right line (indicated by dotted lines) and the second beat occurs on the left-right line.[9]

Figure 5-2 Two Pattern As It Frequently Occurs

The Three-Beat Pattern

The basic three-beat pattern[10] is given in figure 5-3. The motion of the pattern is downward on beat 1, out to the right on beat 2, up and to the center for beat 3.

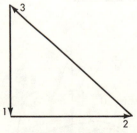

Figure 5-3 Basic Pattern: Three Beats per Measure

The three-beat pattern employed by many conductors[11] is shown in figure 5-4.

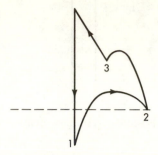

Figure 5-4 Three Pattern As It Frequently Occurs

Attention should be given to beat 2's occurrence on the left-right line. Also notice that in most cases beat 1 is given below the left-right line, and at all times beat 3 is given above the left-right line.

The Four-Beat Pattern

Figure 5-5 indicates the basic patterns of motion for music with meters having four beats.[12] This pattern includes a downward motion for beat 1, motion across the body (to the left) for beat 2, out to the right for the third beat, and up and to the center for beat 4. A typical four-beat pattern[13] is shown in figure 5-6.

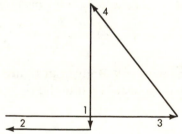

Figure 5-5 Basic Pattern: Four Beats per Measure

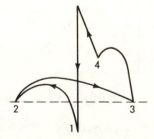

Figure 5-6 Four Pattern As It Frequently Occurs

Attention should be given to the following:

1. In most circumstances, beat 1 occurs below the left-right line.
2. In all patterns, beats 2 and 3 occur on the left-right line.
3. In all situations, beat 4 occurs above the left-right line.

The Six-Beat Pattern

There are two basic styles of beating time in six.[14] They are given in figure 5-7.

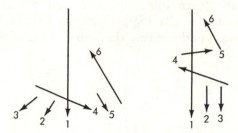

Figure 5-7 Two Basic Patterns: Six Beats per Measure

The typical patterns resulting from these basic ones are shown in figure 5-8.

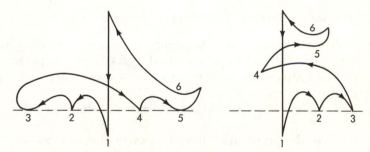

Figure 5-8 Six Patterns As They Frequently Occur

Note that in both patterns the most distinct motion occurs in beats 1 and 4—emphasizing two divisions of three beats each in a measure.[15]

Caution: *The task analysis continues.*

Preparations

The successful beginning of a piece is a most important task of the conductor.

In all starts [preparations] the conductor's motions must indicate the following:

1. the exact moment at which the piece is to commence
2. tempo
3. mood (volume, etc.).[16]

The beat of preparation is given one full beat before the music begins.[17] For example, a musical example in $\frac{4}{4}$, beginning on the first beat, would necessitate a preparatory beat on beat four of a nonexistent measure preceding the first written measure (see figure 5-9). It is usually helpful for the conductor to count a measure or two silently before giving the preparation. In the $\frac{4}{4}$ example just mentioned, the conductor might count three beats silently, give the preparatory beat on beat four of the nonexistent measure, and indicate the appropriate tempo and style of the music that follows.

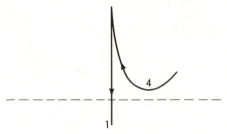

Figure 5-9 Preparatory Beat on Beat Four of $\frac{4}{4}$ Gesture

A lack of confidence shown by beginning conductors in giving preparatory beats will result in lack of a unified attack from the performing ensemble. The preparation must be given with confidence and certain air of authority.

The following are important characteristics according to Green:

1. The speed of the preparation must be exactly the same as the tempo of the piece.
2. The size of the preparatory beat is usually gauged by the loudness of the following dynamic—the larger the preparation, the louder the sound.
3. The style of the preparatory beat should set the mood of the music.[18]

Precision in Attack

A good preparation by the conductor is needed to ensure a precise attack by the musical group. Student conductors should practice giving preparations for a number of musical examples in order to coordinate their right-hand motion. This practice should be done at home, or in a private room, so that the student can gain the necessary confidence before facing a live group. Sometimes individual work in front of a mirror helps to observe and eliminate obvious mistakes of imprecision.

Beginning on Internal Beats

The preparations discussed above began on the last beat of a nonexistent measure with the actual music starting on the first beat of the measure. The general rule that applied to that example applies to beats within the measure: the preparation is given one full beat before the actual beat on which the music begins. Figure 5-10 shows examples of preparatory beats.[19]

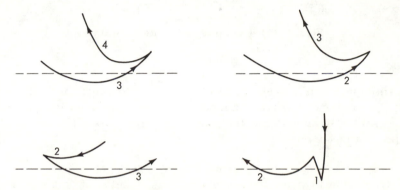

Figure 5-10 Examples of Preparatory Beat Gestures

The patterns in figure 5-10 can serve as models in meters other than those listed if the correct substitution is made for the actual preparation desired.

The preparatory beat receives greater authority and gives greater emphasis if other procedures are incorporated with the correct right-hand motion. The conductor should take a breath with the musicians as part of the preparation and attack—inhaling on the preparatory beat and exhaling on the attack. A raised or upward gesture as part of the preparation will help give an invitation to play. Also, a nod of the head on the beat of attack will help secure a precise entrance.

Sometimes a double preparation will occur with beginning students, especially when the first beat is the preparatory beat. Student conductors should be careful to make the movement straight down when using beat one as a preparatory beat.

Releases (Cut-offs)

There are a number of effective gestures used for releasing the sound. The actual gesture used depends on the point in the pattern where the release should occur as well as stylistic concerns including phrase endings, dynamics, etc. Green[20] gives the following suggested gestures for cut-offs (see figure 5-11):

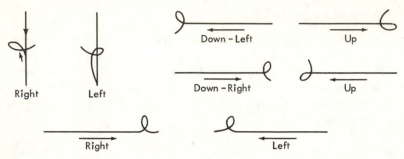

Figure 5-11 Examples of Release Gestures

Tempo

Although tempo is a relative term and never remains absolutely constant,[21] a conductor must have a specific tempo in mind before confronting a group. Green suggests the following process to help develop the tempo of a piece:

1. Check the composer's indications: Allegro, Adagio, Moderato.
2. Sing the melody line. Try several variations of tempo within the broad outline designated by the composer. Certainly one of them will make the melody sound "as it should."
3. Glance through the composition, noting especially the faster notes and making sure that they are playable at the chosen tempo.[22]

As pointed out above, actual performance tempos rarely remain perfectly constant. Students with obvious rhythmic problems should feel at ease practicing with a metronome, without undue concern over a mechanistic performance.

Changes in Tempo

After basic tempo decisions have been made, judgments concerning changes of tempo must follow. Many terms indicating changes of tempo occur in various scores. The conductor must have a complete understanding of these terms and of the composer's wishes in a particular piece. The conductor is responsible for directing the players as a unit through the indicated tempo changes. The following are areas of concern in tempo changes according to Ross:

1. Clarity of beat is of great importance in ensuring precision of ensemble.

2. The conductor must catch everyone's attention at the beginning of a tempo change. This may be accomplished by such techniques as: altering the size of the beat; making a large gesture; changing stance; using the left hand if it has been at rest; moving the right hand and baton directly in front to take command.[23]

No matter what techniques are used to indicate a change of tempo, it is important that the conductor actually feels the change of pulse as it occurs. In sudden changes of tempo, the new tempo must be shown clearly without any anticipation occurring in the tempo of the previous section. If there is a pause in the music between sudden changes of tempo, the last beat before the change is given in the new tempo as a preparation.

Fermatas

A fermata can occur in a number of different situations in a score. Each situation presents a slightly different technical problem to the conductor. The execution of fermatas is a difficult situation for beginning, as well as experienced, conductors.

"The fermata is held out as a sustained tone with no rhythmic pulsation . . . it is a cessation of rhythm."[24] It is the responsibility of the conductor to decide the length of the fermata based on the musical context. Usually, the baton moves slowly throughout the fermata, but occasionally the note is held with a stationary, intense gesture, or sometimes with a definite shaking of the stick. In some cases the left hand may be used to give the sustaining motion. The conductor must determine the proper gesture warranted by the music. The end of the fermata must be indicated by a release and followed by a preparation for the continuing music. Sometimes a single gesture can serve as both the release and preparation.[25]

Caution: *Isn't this task analysis long?*

Dynamics

Loud and Soft

Generally, dynamics are indicated by the size of beat—larger gestures for loud music and smaller gestures for soft music. However, the conductor must incorporate the entire body—arm, hands, shoulders, face, eyes—in expressing dynamics. It is the conductor's responsibility to produce the dynamic level that is indicated by the composer rather than just giving gestures that represent what is being played by the performers.

It is necessary for beginning conductors to practice indicating dynamics through gestures before stepping in front of a group. Again, it may be helpful to use a mirror while conducting imaginary dynamic levels, or a pianist in some specific exercises.[26]

Use of Left Hand

The left hand should be used as a support for the actions of the right hand. The left hand may be used to help indicate dynamics, as well as cues, entrances, releases, preparations, phrasing, and accents.[27]

The left hand may indicate sustained dynamic levels as well as changing dynamics. When performing a loud passage, the palm of the left hand faces upward or inward, and the fingers are somewhat bent.[28] In a soft passage the palm of the left hand faces outward toward the performing group.

Accents

Accents are indicated by various signs and terms in a composition. The conductor should have a firm understanding of how the accents in a particular piece are to be performed and must communicate this understanding to the players. The accented notes are conducted within the pattern and style of the composition, with more emphasis placed on the accented beats.[29]

Changing Dynamics

According to Rudolf,[30] changes of dynamics are indicated by the following:

1. Changing the size of the beat (as explained above).
2. Using the left hand. Palm upward or inward for forte; palm outward for piano. A crescendo is indicated by lifting the left hand, palm facing upward from hip level to eye level. For decrescendo, the hand is turned to palm facing the performers and then is dropped. In both the crescendo and the decrescendo, timing depends on the musical context.
3. Moving the right hand nearer to, or farther away from the body. To emphasize a loud beat the right hand may move away from the body. Likewise, a retreat of the right hand to a position closer to the body makes a soft passage more effective.

Style

Legato and Staccato

The motion connecting the beats indicates the type of articulation desired. Legato music should be shown by very smooth and connected gestures. The motion in conducting legato should be continuous and uniform. Rudolf describes legato conducting in this manner:

The espressivo-legato beat is a curved, continuous motion. It is done with a certain tension in the forearm. The intensity and degree of curve vary with the emotional quality of the music. The size may be anywhere from fairly small to very large.[31]

Staccato music is shown with a "flick" of the baton on the beats and with as little motions as possible between the beats.[32] The connecting motion between staccato beats should be quickly done. Rudolf offers a good description of staccato conducting:

The light-staccato beat is a quick, straight motion with a stop on each count. The gestures are small. The full-staccato beat is a quick, slightly curved motion with a stop on each count. It is snappy and energetic, with a characteristic "bouncing" on the down-beat. The size may vary from small to large.[33]

Use of Left Hand

The left hand may be used to help indicate stylistic concerns and can be especially useful in indicating changes of style.

Marcato

In conducting marcato music each beat must be "marked" or stressed. The gesture should be heavy or weighty in character. "This kind of motion is related to 'staccato' conducting but uses a slower, more emphatic movement between beats".[34] Rudolf describes marcato conducting in this manner:

The marcato beat is a heavy motion with a stop on each count. It is forceful, sometimes aggressive in character and medium to large in size. The gestures connecting the counts are slower than in staccato; they are either straight or curved (espressivo) depending on the music.[35]

Cueing

Cueing is a technique that gives a direction or instruction to a performer or section. A cue is usually given to the appropriate person, or persons, as they begin playing after a series of rests.

Basically, cues are given in three ways: with the eyes, with the baton, and with the left hand. Green suggests the following manners of giving a cue:

1. By the baton, in the manner of a time-beating gesture directed specifically toward a player or group of players. . . .
2. By the left hand, in a special motion (not a time-beating gesture), sometimes with a preparation gesture preceding the cue and sometimes just an indication on the beat-point.

3. By the eyes, a lift of the eyebrows or a nod of the head. This last is used in very quiet passages where anything other than the most subtle of motions would disrupt the mood. These gestures are also used when both hands are already fully occupied with other necessary conductorial gestures.
4. The two hands should not cross over each other in giving cues.[36]

As to the manner of executing a cue, Ross states that the "conductor should establish eye contact with the musicians before the beat on which the event takes place and then give the cue with the hand or baton between his or her eyes and theirs."[37] Generally all cues should have a one-beat preparatory gesture.

Complex passages sometimes require rapid, successive cues. If this problem arises, the conductor should prepare the first cue and then use each cueing gesture as preparation for successive entrances. In some complex passages the conductor may have to choose only the more important cues and maintain a precise beat pattern allowing the musicians to determine their own entrances.

Eye Contact

The importance of score memorization cannot be overemphasized. Score memorization gives the conductor the opportunity for maximum eye contact with the performing group. In your observations, count eye contact as occurring correctly *only* if it continues for three or more seconds.

Following the development of operational definitions, a technique for assessment of these skill categories must be developed and tested. In the above example of conducting technique, videotape is a useful tool for assessment. The videotape equipment set-up, diagrammed in Appendix N, can be the basis of a highly reliable technique for student and teacher observation and evaluation of conducting practicums. Using a simple system of sampling conducting behavior in each of the eight skill categories, and marking each time whether the behavior within that category was correct or incorrect based on the operational definitions, the observer can develop an overall picture of conducting competency. If one could characterize each of the eight skill categories as equally important and effective in communicating an affective response to the performing group and/or audience, then one would hope that the percentage of correct responses would be equally high for all categories. Indeed it would seem difficult to imagine a high level of affective response occurring to the optimum level with an extreme weakness or absence of skill development in any one of the eight categories.

After the assessment tool has been developed and used without alteration, an evaluation of it is in order. This might involve having students observe each others' videotapes and comparing student reliability or agreement concerning correct and incorrect responses. It might also involve the instructor's observing the students' videotapes and computing reliability or agreement between himself or herself and the student.

Thus, after tasks have been carefully analyzed, the music educator should systematically investigate the effectiveness of students' progress. The following traditional research model provides an excellent basis for describing the efforts of the experimenting teacher.

Caution: *See how elaborate and detailed a complex task is to analyze?*

2. Record (Pretest)

Students were music education and music majors enrolled in a basic conducting class. This was the first conducting experience for all students. The time period for the course was one semester (fourteen two-hour class periods).

Baseline scores were established in each of the eight categories (beat patterns, preparations, releases, tempo, dynamics, style, cueing, and eye contact) through a pretest. Each student was videotaped conducting one four-measure example in each of the following meters: $\frac{2}{4}$; $\frac{3}{4}$; $\frac{4}{4}$; and $\frac{6}{8}$ (in 6). Examples were given to students one week prior to the test with the following instructions:

> These four-measure examples should demonstrate your knowledge of (a) beginning, continuing, and stopping a conducting pattern; (b) establishing speed or tempo; (c) indicating musical style and dynamics through appropriate conducting gestures; and (d) entrance cueing through eye contact, body movement, and use of the left hand.

Videotaped examples were then graded by three instructors using the operational definitions to be given to students and the musical indications in the examples.

Categories of beat patterns, tempo, style, dynamics, and eye contact were judged "correct" or "incorrect" for each measure conducted. Categories of preparation, release, and cueing were judged "correct" or "incorrect" for each occurrence. Reliability among the three instructors was .98 as calculated by the formula: agreements divided by agreements plus disagreements. A percentage of correct responses for each student in each of the eight skill categories was then computed. Results were as follows:

Table 5-1 Percentages of Correct Student Pretest Responses

Category	Mean Percentage Correct
Beat Patterns	10.94
Tempo	39.94
Dynamics	20.94
Style	27.17
Eye Contact	2.67
Cueing	1.50
Preparations	5.22
Releases	35.22

As can be observed, data demonstrated less than 50% correct responses in all eight categories.

3. Consequate (Teaching Technique)

Following the pretest (record), students conducted one five-minute and two eight-minute practicums using beat patterns in two and four and one five-minute and two eight-minute practicums using beat patterns in three and six. Basic conducting skills were taught by asking students to pay attention to (a) five of the eight categories (beat patterns, preparations, releases, tempo, and eye contact) for practicums one and four; (b) seven of the eight categories (beat patterns, preparations, releases, tempo, eye contact, dynamics, and cueing) for practicums two and five; and (c) all eight categories (beat patterns, preparations, releases, tempo, eye contact, dynamics, cueing, and style) for practicums three and six. Following the sixth practicum, baseline was again measured through a posttest.

Practicums

Six conducting practicums were assigned to each student as outlined above. During the practicums students practiced their conducting technique in the eight skill categories. Students were told not to interact verbally with the group. They were instructed to indicate everything through conducting gestures (except for page and measure numbers). Students were also sensitized to observing musical indications in the score (dynamics, style, tempo, phrasing, etc.) and to transfer these indications to conducting gestures rather than by talking.

The time period allotted to each practicum was divided in half with the first half devoted to practice in one meter and the second half to practice in the other meter. For example, for practicum one, students practiced conducting a score in two for 2½ minutes. They were then told to "change" at which point they practiced conducting a score in four for 2½ minutes. The eight-minute practicum was divided so that four minutes of practice in each meter was possible.

Music for the practicums was selected from *Five Centuries of Choral Music* (Schirmer) and specific pieces were assigned to each student. Additional octavos were selected for $\frac{6}{8}$ examples. Criteria for the selection of music were based on their usefulness in the development of skill in each of the eight categories. Criteria were as follows:

> Musical examples must include (1) opportunities for cueing; (2) dynamic contrasts; (3) tempo problems including fermatas, caesuras, ritards, rallentandos; (4) no meter changes; (5) preparations occurring not only at the beginning of the piece but also within, preparations for changes in dynamics or recommencing after a fermata; (6) releases occurring not only at the end of the piece but also within, e.g., releases for phrasing; (7) opportunities for two or more style gestures.

Following each practicum students observed themselves using the following observation forms developed for the course (see figures 5-12 and 5-13). Following practicums one and four students observed the categories of beat pattern, preparation, release, tempo and eye contact, marking each category "correct" (+) or "incorrect" (−) every fifteen seconds. After practicums two and five they observed the categories beat pattern, preparation, release, tempo, eye contact, dynamics, and cueing in the same manner; and after practicums three and six all categories were observed and marked "correct" or "incorrect."

To help students become more accurate in self-observation, each student was required to have a reliability observer and to participate as a reliability observer for each practicum.

Operational definitions and musical indications in the score were the basis for marking "correct" and "incorrect" responses in each category. Reliability was computed using the same formula as in the pretest. Students were required to achieve a minimum of 75% agreement. In addition to student/student reliability, student/teacher reliability was computed for each practicum. A comparison of these reliability quotients follows:

Table 5-2 Reliability Quotient of Practicum Scores

Practicum	Student/Student	Teacher/Student
I	.87	.65
II	.93	.69
III	.92	.88
IV	.91	.88
V	.93	.96
VI	.94	.95

NAME_____ DATE_____ RELIABILITY OBSERVER_____

SELECTION_____ METER(S)_____

Int.	Beat Pattern	Tempo	Dynamics	Style	Eye Contact
1	+ —	+ —	+ —	+ —	+ —
2	+ —	+ —	+ —	+ —	+ —
3	+ —	+ —	+ —	+ —	+ —
4	+ —	+ —	+ —	+ —	+ —
5	+ —	+ —	+ —	+ —	+ —
6	+ —	+ —	+ —	+ —	+ —
7	+ —	+ —	+ —	+ —	+ —
8	+ —	+ —	+ —	+ —	+ —
9	+ —	+ —	+ —	+ —	+ —
10	+ —	+ —	+ —	+ —	+ —
11	+ —	+ —	+ —	+ —	+ —
12	+ —	+ —	+ —	+ —	+ —
13	+ —	+ —	+ —	+ —	+ —
14	+ —	+ —	+ —	+ —	+ —
15	+ —	+ —	+ —	+ —	+ —
16	+ —	+ —	+ —	+ —	+ —
17	+ —	+ —	+ —	+ —	+ —
18	+ —	+ —	+ —	+ —	+ —
19	+ —	+ —	+ —	+ —	+ —
20	+ —	+ —	+ —	+ —	+ —
21	+ —	+ —	+ —	+ —	+ —
22	+ —	+ —	+ —	+ —	+ —
23	+ —	+ —	+ —	+ —	+ —
24	+ —	+ —	+ —	+ —	+ —
25	+ —	+ —	+ —	+ —	+ —
26	+ —	+ —	+ —	+ —	+ —
27	+ —	+ —	+ —	+ —	+ —
28	+ —	+ —	+ —	+ —	+ —
29	+ —	+ —	+ —	+ —	+ —
30	+ —	+ —	+ —	+ —	+ —
31	+ —	+ —	+ —	+ —	+ —
32	+ —	+ —	+ —	+ —	+ —

(Row groupings at left: 1–4 = **1**, 5–8 = **2**, 9–12 = **3**, 13–16 = **4**, 17–20 = **5**, 21–24 = **6**, 25–28 = **7**, 29–32 = **8**)

TOTALS: Beat Patterns   +____ —____ % correct_____

Tempo   +____ —____ % correct_____

Dynamics   +____ —____ % correct_____

Style   +____ —____ % correct_____

Eye Contact   +____ —____ % correct_____

RELIABILITY: Agreements —_____ Disagreements —_____

% Agreements —_____

Figure 5-12 Conducting Technique Observation Form I

Int.	Preparation			Release			Cueing		
	Eye Contact	Body Mvt.	Gesture	Eye Contact	Body Mvt.	Gesture	Eye Contact	Body Mvt.	Gesture
1	+ −	+ −	+ −	+ −	+ −	+ −	+ −	+ −	+ −
2	+ −	+ −	+ −	+ −	+ −	+ −	+ −	+ −	+ −
3	+ −	+ −	+ −	+ −	+ −	+ −	+ −	+ −	+ −
4	+ −	+ −	+ −	+ −	+ −	+ −	+ −	+ −	+ −
5	+ −	+ −	+ −	+ −	+ −	+ −	+ −	+ −	+ −
6	+ −	+ −	+ −	+ −	+ −	+ −	+ −	+ −	+ −
7	+ −	+ −	+ −	+ −	+ −	+ −	+ −	+ −	+ −
8	+ −	+ −	+ −	+ −	+ −	+ −	+ −	+ −	+ −
9	+ −	+ −	+ −	+ −	+ −	+ −	+ −	+ −	+ −
10	+ −	+ −	+ −	+ −	+ −	+ −	+ −	+ −	+ −
11	+ −	+ −	+ −	+ −	+ −	+ −	+ −	+ −	+ −
12	+ −	+ −	+ −	+ −	+ −	+ −	+ −	+ −	+ −

TOTALS:

Preparation

Eye Contact: + ___ − ___ ___ %+

Body Mvt.: + ___ − ___ ___ %+

Gesture: + ___ − ___ ___ %+

Cueing

Eye Contact: + ___ − ___ ___ %+

Body Mvt.: + ___ − ___ ___ %+

Gesture: + ___ − ___ ___ %+

Release

Eye Contact: + ___ − ___ ___ %+

Body Mvt.: + ___ − ___ ___ %+

Gesture: + ___ − ___ ___ %+

Reliability

Eye Contact: + ___ − ___ ___ %+

Body Mvt.: + ___ − ___ ___ %+

Gesture: + ___ − ___ ___ %+

Figure 5-13 Conducting Technique Observation Form II

117

Thus, videotape feedback provided a means for students to analyze their conducting in comparison with operational definitions provided by the instructor and musical indications in the score. In addition, the student with the help of a reliability observer was able to determine percentages of correct responses within each of the categories assigned for a practicum. A further teacher/student reliability check provided feedback concerning whether the student understood the operational definitions as the teacher intended.

Following the third and sixth practicums, students wrote a self-critique (see Appendix O for an example of a student critique) based on data collected during videotaped observations. The first critique compared practicums one, two, and three; the second compared practicums four, five, and six. Instructions for writing the critiques were as follows:

> The purposes of the conducting critique are to learn to assimilate various kinds of input in a meaningful way and to stimulate growth in conducting technique. Your input for the critique consists of self-evaluation via videotape. Your evaluation will consist of a summary of percentages of correct technique in the following categories: beat pattern, tempo, preparation, release, dynamics, style, cueing, and eye contact. Data will be collected by you and a reliability observer while observing six of your conducting practicums on videotape with behavioral observation forms.
>
> The conducting critique should be typed with correct grammar, spelling, etc. It should contain the following sections: (1) *introductory paragraph* (one or two sentences) containing the semester in which you did your presentation, titles and composers of compositions you rehearsed, and number and length of the practicums to be discussed in this critique; (2) statement discussing *procedures* for collecting data and reliability observation including percentage of agreement for each observation; (3) presentation of *data* without comment (see examples of tabular format); (4) *discussion* of data including categories which need improvement and what kind of improvement is needed as well as problems in understanding operational definitions; and (5) *appendices* containing all observation forms.

Following practicums three and six a group feedback session was held. During each session operational definitions were reviewed and students were given the opportunity to ask questions. Musical indications in each score were reviewed. Videotapes of practicums three and six were shown and students discussed positive aspects of their conducting. Each feedback session was approximately two hours long. No instruction or reinforcement was given during the practicums.

> **Caution:** *Do you think that the practicums represent the best way to teach conducting skills? How would you have done it?*

4. Evaluate (Process and Product)

Evaluation within a competency-based instructional sequence should focus on two areas. First, the *product* of the instructional sequence should be evaluated. A product evaluation involves an assessment of the level of expertise attained by students at the end of the instructional sequence. It is important that students are required to transfer skills to several new situations before a final product evaluation occurs. In this study, product evaluation consisted of a comparison of pre- versus posttest scores (percentages of correct responses) in each of the eight categories. Also, student attitude was assessed through the administration of the Evaluation of Music Instruction form (Appendix Q).

Second, the *process* of the instructional sequence should be evaluated to determine strengths and weaknesses upon which to base future course revisions. To achieve this kind of evaluation, continuous recording of student progress must take place. Weekly, biweekly, monthly achievement checks should be made. In this study, the process evaluation consisted of a comparison of data from pretest, practicums one through six, and posttest. This data represented percentages of correct responses in each of the eight categories outlined previously. In addition to achievement data, student attitude toward their achievement was elicited twice in the form of written critiques.

Three expert judges determined correct/incorrect responses for each measure of pre- and posttest conducting examples across eight categories (beat patterns, tempo, dynamics, cueing, preparations, releases, style, and eye contact). Averages of correct responses for pretest, posttest, and pre-/posttest gain scores are shown in the following table:

Table 5-3 Averages of Correct Responses for Pretest and Posttest

Category	Pretest %	Posttest %	Gain %
Beat Patterns	10.94	84.11	73.17
Tempo	39.94	84.33	44.39
Dynamics	20.94	59.78	38.84
Cueing	1.50	82.83	81.33
Preparations	5.22	90.17	84.95
Releases	35.22	86.06	50.84
Style	27.17	78.39	51.22
Eye Contact	2.67	89.22	86.55

Also, student perceptions of instruction were assessed by items in the Evaluation of Music Instruction instrument (Appendix Q).

The following graph (see figure 5-14) shows that during the pretest, students were achieving less than 50% correct responses in any of the eight categories. As they proceeded through the first three practicums, the effectiveness of the successive approximations teaching procedure is evident as the categories consequated for the first practicum (beat pattern, tempo, preparations, releases, and eye contact) increase in accuracy. Appreciable increases in accuracy for dynamics and cueing (consequated for practicum two) and style (consequated for practicum three) are also demonstrated in the graph. It should be noted, in addition, that by practicum three students were achieving above 70% accuracy in all eight categories.

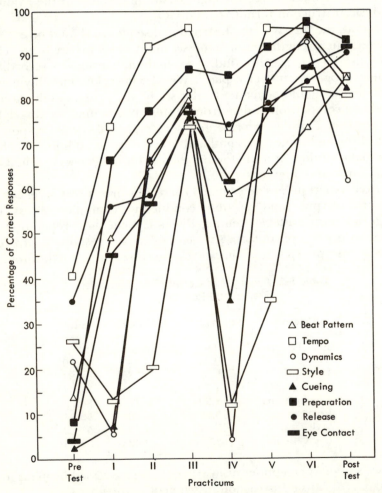

Figure 5-14 Percentages of Correct Responses in Conducting Technique for Pretest, Practicums, and Posttest

For practicum four (during which students had to transfer conducting skills to different beat patterns and different musical scores) a "classic" return to baseline is demonstrated for the skill categories of style and dynamics. For all other categories it would appear that some transfer of learning occurred. The effectiveness of the successive approximations teaching procedure is again shown by the graph for practicums four, five, and six. By practicum six students are again achieving above 70% correct responses in all eight categories. Finally the graph shows that transfer of skills to the posttest occurred with no return to baseline for any of eight categories. This transfer involved using all beat patterns (2, 3, 4, and 6) for different musical scores.

Caution: *Did you stay somewhat detached from the subject matter? Skim through the past example one more time and notice only the broad categories: PINPOINT, RECORD, CONSEQUATE, EVALUATE.*

5. Setting Competencies for Yourself and Others

The advent of performance or competency-based teacher education and certification has prompted music educators to reexamine university and public school music curricula and to devise behavioral objectives which can be observed and measured. Teachers must now provide evidence of student achievement, attentiveness, and attitude as well as evidence of their own skills in presenting subject matter, maintaining discipline, and managing classrooms. For music educators who are accustomed to dealing with apparently abstract and intangible aesthetic and creative experiences in music, the demands of a competency-based approach seem both difficult and confusing.

The successful teacher is one who can define *a priori* values regarding all aspects of teaching. Value areas in teaching which need constant definition and evaluation include the use of time, social and academic interaction with students and others, and the selection and use of methods and materials. After values have been articulated, skilled overt behaviors (competencies) must be developed to teach or to do those things which are valued. In other words, the teacher must now *act* in a significant way.

The teacher as actor must master overt behavior to direct the valued learning process in students. Just as the virtuoso violinist must practice difficult musical passages painstakingly, so the virtuoso teacher must practice effective overt behavior, analysis of the behavior of students, and techniques of reinforcement. This constant practice must begin in student teaching and continue throughout the teaching career. Hopefully, the end product will be a music teacher who not only improves as a result of continued self-assessment but a person who takes joy in knowing that students' lives are richer because of a finer music experience.

One of the greatest joys of teaching is that one will always be learning and changing. There is continued vitality through constant observation, analysis, and evaluation, not only of oneself but also of one's students.

It may be assumed that most people enter the teaching profession because they *care* about (value) a subject matter or an idea. However, simply to *care* is not enough. Without some overt behavioral demonstration of caring, others will not know that caring is taking place and, therefore, learning will not take place. Teachers' values, or the things they care about, must constantly be made plain if others are to be affected by them.

NOTES

[1]W. Robert Houston and Robert B. Howsam, eds., *Competency-Based Teacher Education: Progress, Problems, and Prospects* (Chicago: Science Research Associates, Inc., 1972).

[2]Charles H. Madsen, Jr. and Clifford K. Madsen, *Teaching/Discipline: A Positive Approach for Educational Development,* expanded 2nd ed. for professionals (Boston: Allyn and Bacon, 1974).

[3]Alan A. Ross, *Techniques for Beginning Conductors* (Belmont, Calif.: Wadsworth Publishing Company, 1976), p. 10.

[4]Elizabeth A. H. Green, *The Modern Conductor* (Englewood Cliffs, N.J.: Prentice-Hall, Inc., 1969). Brock McElheran, *Conducting Techniques* (New York: Oxford University Press, 1966). Alan A. Ross, *Techniques for Beginning Conductors* (Belmont, Calif.: Wadsworth Publishing Company, 1976). Max Rudolf, *The Grammar of Conducting* (New York: G. Schirmer, Inc., 1950).

[5]Green, *The Modern Conductor,* p. 7.

[6]Green, *The Modern Conductor,* pp. 8–12.

[7]Ross, *Techniques for Beginning Conductors,* pp. 2–3.

[8]Ross, *Techniques for Beginning Conductors,* p. 62.

[9]Rudolf, *The Grammar of Conducting,* p. 70.

[10]Ross, *Techniques for Beginning Conductors,* p. 35.

[11]Green, *The Modern Conductor,* p. 26.

[12]Ross, *Techniques for Beginning Conductors,* p. 3.

[13]Green, *The Modern Conductor,* p. 28.

[14]Ross, *Techniques for Beginning Conductors,* pp. 157, 159.

[15]Ross, *Techniques for Beginning Conductors,* pp. 157, 158.

[16]McElheran, *Conducting Techniques,* p. 64.

[17]Rudolf, *The Grammar of Conducting,* p. 10.

[18]Green, *The Modern Conductor,* p. 15.

[19]Ross, *Techniques for Beginning Conductors,* pp. 35, 55, 57.

[20]Green, *The Modern Conductor,* p. 17.

[21]Ross, *Techniques for Beginning Conductors,* p. 253.

[22]Green, *The Modern Conductor,* p. 18.

[23]Ross, *Techniques for Beginning Conductors,* p. 253.

[24]Green, *The Modern Conductor,* p. 92.

[25]For detailed discussions of conducting fermatas, see Green, *The Modern Conductor,* pp. 92–105 and Ross, *Techniques for Beginning Conductors,* pp. 311–18.

[26]Exercises for practice may be found in Ross, *Techniques for Beginning Conductors,* pp. 39–41, and McElheran, *Conducting Techniques,* pp. 39–40.

[27]Exercises for practice may be found in Ross, *Techniques for Beginning Conductors,* p. 125, and Green, *The Modern Conductor,* pp. 87–90.

[28]Rudolf, *The Grammar of Conducting,* p. 27.

[29]Exercises for practicing accented beats are given in Ross, *Techniques for Beginning Conductors,* pp. 173–74. and McElheran, *Conducting Techniques,* p. 41.

[30]Rudolf, *The Grammar of Conducting,* pp. 52–54, 58–60.

[31]Rudolf, *The Grammar of Conducting,* p. 24.

[32]Ross, *Techniques for Beginning Conductors,* p. 106.

[33]Rudolf, *The Grammar of Conducting,* pp. 16, 19.

[34]Ross, *Techniques for Beginning Conductors,* p. 150.

[35]Rudolf, *The Grammar of Conducting,* p. 91.

[36]Green, *The Modern Conductor,* p. 87.

[37]Ross, *Techniques for Beginning Conductors,* p. 71.

Appendices

AUTHOR'S NOTE

The following appendices contain suggestions for resource file development, lesson and rehearsal planning, and student progress records. Suggestions for evaluation are also provided. These suggestions are made to facilitate the adoption of practices of constant record-keeping and evaluation of the teaching/learning process by both student teachers and beginning teachers who will be using this textbook. Appendix A is a suggested guide for field experiences based on material contained in this text. Goals and assignments are an outgrowth of the authors' conceptions of an effective introduction to the art and science of teaching. The extended field experience outline has been successfully used for an internship with student teachers who were in the final term of the senior year. However, each goal and its accompanying assignments could be effectively used separately as one-day, one-week, or more than one-week field experiences. As has been previously noted in the text, one of the characteristics of competency-based music education is the importance of field experiences throughout the undergraduate teacher preparation program as well as in the in-service training of beginning teachers.

APPENDIX A

OUTLINE OF EXTENDED FIELD EXPERIENCES
FOR STUDENT AND BEGINNING TEACHERS

Pinpoints:

1. To understand the values of a school system through the investigation of (a) the role of guidance and the guidance counselor in the school system; (b) the administrative organization of the school system; (c) grading; (d) schoolwide testing programs; (e) accountability; (f) the total curriculum; (g) school services; i.e., the library, audio-visual, health, cafeteria, custodial; (h) teacher organization; (i) visiting specialists; (j) grouping of students; and (k) team teaching.
2. To increase knowledge of choral and instrumental literature as well as materials for use in elementary and secondary schools through developing a comprehensive resource file, structuring conversations with experienced teachers, and compiling annotated sheets or cards.
3. To develop a positive approach to teaching through systematic observation.
4. To develop skill in teaching/rehearsing through (a) restructuring personal and professional use of time by keeping and analyzing time logs; (b) experimenting with techniques in the management of inappropriate pupil and class behavior by pinpointing, recording, consequating, and evaluating those behaviors; and (c) thoughtful planning and discussion with a master teacher, lesson presentation, and subsequent analysis and evaluation of the lesson with a master teacher.
5. To develop techniques in the long-term course and rehearsal planning through use of a behavioral model (pinpoint, record, consequate, and evaluate).
6. To increase achievement and/or performance level of students in classes and/or rehearsals through audiotape and videotape recordings and subsequent evaluation.

7. To practice teaching at different levels (elementary, middle school, junior high, and senior high school) and in different music areas (choral, instrumental, music theory, music history, and humanities).

Record:

A videotape and/or audiotape recording is made of the student or beginning teacher at (a) an initial rehearsal of a composition to be rehearsed solely by that teacher; and/or (b) the first class or lesson taught for a unit or solo preparation (see Appendix N for equipment set-up). Subsequent analysis of the videotape and/or audiotape is then made by the student/beginning teacher and master teacher using evaluation procedures described in Chapter Four

Other evaluations consist of (a) assessment of written reports submitted by student and beginning teachers; (b) examination of lesson, course, or rehearsal plans; (c) analysis of data collected by student and beginning teachers through observation, time logs, and pinpointing exercises; (d) examination of the resource file; and (e) periodic ratings of student and beginning teachers made by master teachers and pupils using rating sheets (see Appendices I, J, K, L, M, P, and Q).

Consequate (Refer to Academic Calendar):

1. Orientation (See Chapter One):

a. Explore physical plant and meet significant people.
b. Interview the guidance counselor.
c. Complete school services, evaluation, measurement, and school organization reports.

2. Resource File Development (See Chapter Two):

a. Submit written summaries of at least seven *structured* conversations with master teachers.
b. Complete at least five annotated file cards per week.

3. Observation Sequence

Complete as follows (see Chapter Three):

a. Music classes, approximately four hours: 3 Student Observation Form C's; 3 Teacher Observation Form A's; 3 Choral Rehearsal Observation Forms; 3 Instrumental Rehearsal Observation Forms; 4 Music Conductor Observation Forms.

b. Nonmusic classes, approximately two hours: 3 Student Observation Form C's; 3 Teacher Observation Form A's. (*Note: Elementary teachers should substitute four Elementary Music Observation Forms and four Student Observation Form C's.)

4. *Design and Management of Musical Learning (see Chapter Four):*

a. Time organization: Time Log A—Personal time—follow instructions Chapter Four; Time Log B—professional time—complete one per week.
b. Complete four pinpoint exercises demonstrating ability to manage inappropriate group and individual pupil behavior (refer to Chapters Three and Four for techniques and suggestions).
c. Keep daily lesson and/or rehearsal plans using forms provided in Chapter Four (see also Appendices E, F, and G) in a loose-leaf binder: also keep progress charts for each student you teach on an individual basis.

5. *Course or Rehearsal Plan:*

Design a course or rehearsal plan for a three-week period; include a detailed task analysis (pinpoint), record-evaluate procedure, and consequate (teaching procedure); a videotape/audiotape will be made at the beginning and end of the three-week period (see Chapter Five).

6. *Evaluations:*

Have a master teacher and students evaluate you as follows:

a. Master teachers—one Weekly Music Teaching Evaluation per week.
b. Students—an attitude survey (see Appendices K, L, and M) at the end of a course unit or rehearsal sequence with a summary of the results.

Evaluate (*See* **Record**):

Competency levels should be determined by college supervisors, master teachers, school administrators, and student/beginning teachers working in consortium.

APPENDIX B

ACADEMIC CALENDAR—EXTENDED FIELD EXPERIENCES

One of the characteristics of competency-based teacher education concerns the achievement of competencies in a field setting. The field experiences outlined in the text and in Appendix A may be used in a variety of ways. To facilitate creativity in their usage, the following calendar provides a completion time period for each of the field experiences. (Refer to Appendix A for specific assignments.)

ACADEMIC CALENDAR
SEVEN-WEEK EXTENDED FIELD EXPERIENCE

Week 1, Day 1	Day 2
O R I E N T A T I O N	
	School Services Report
Day 3	Day 4
Conversation with Master Teacher Interview Guidance Counselor	Evaluation, Measurement, School Organization Reports
Day 5	Week 2, Day 6
5 Annotated Cards Complete Weekly Music Teaching Evaluation Complete	Day 1 – Day 5 Assignments due Begin Time Log A
Day 7	
Continue Time Log A	Consequate Time Log A
O B S E R V A T I O N	

Day 9 Conversation with Master Teacher Resume Time Log A	**Day 10** 5 Annotated Cards Complete Continue Time Log A Weekly Music Teaching Evaluation Complete

O B S E R V A T I O N

Week 3, Day 11 Time Log A Report due	**Day 12** Begin 1st Pinpoint
Day 12 Conversation with Master Teacher	**Day 14** Begin work on course unit or rehearsal sequence
Day 15 5 Annotated Cards Complete Weekly Music Teaching Evaluation Complete	**Week 4, Day 16** Begin Time Log B 1st Pinpoint Due Lesson Plan Book Due
Day 17 Begin 2nd Pinpoint	**Day 18**
Day 19 Conversation with Master Teacher	**Day 20** 5 Annotated Cards Complete Weekly Music Teaching Evaluation Complete
Week 5, Day 21 Time Log B Due 2nd Pinpoint Due Lesson Plan Book Due	**Day 22** Begin 3rd Pinpoint Conversation with Master Teacher

Day 23	Day 24
Day 25 5 Annotated Cards Complete Weekly Music Teaching Evaluation Complete Course/rehearsal unit complete	Week 6, Day 26 Videotaping of first lesson or rehearsal Time Log B Due 3rd Pinpoint Due Lesson Plan Book Due
Day 27 Begin 4th Pinpoint	Day 28
Day 29 Conversation with Master Teacher	Day 30 5 Annotated Cards Complete Weekly Music Teaching Evaluation Complete
Week 7, Day 31 Time Log B Due 4th Pinpoint Due Lesson Plan Book Due	Day 32 Conversation with Master Teacher
Day 33	Day 34 Videotaping of final class lesson or rehearsal
Day 35 5 Annotated Cards Complete Weekly Music Teaching Evaluation Complete	

APPENDIX C

CHORAL, INSTRUMENTAL, SOLO MUSIC
ANALYSIS CARD FORMS

CHORAL MUSIC ANALYSIS

Title_____

Composer/Arranger_____

Voice Parts_____Publisher_____

Catalog Number_____ SELECTED   REJECTED

      DIFFICULT   MEDIUM   EASY

Appeal:

Range and tessitura (range notated in white notes; tessitura in black notes)

Text:

Dynamic Range:
Phrase Length:
Melody:

Harmony:

Texture:

Rhythm:

Form:

Accompaniment:

Size of Chorus (Recommendation Only):

The Printed Page:

Other Comments:

INSTRUMENTAL MUSIC ANALYSIS

Title _____

Composer/Arranger _____

Instrumentation _____

Publishers _____

Catalog Number _____   SELECTED   REJECTED

         DIFFICULT   MEDIUM   EASY

Appeal:

Possible range and/or tessitura problems (range notated in white notes; tessitura in black notes)

```
═══════════          ═══════════          ═══════════
───────────          ───────────          ───────────
───────────          ───────────          ───────────
───────────          ───────────          ───────────
═══════════          ═══════════          ═══════════

═══════════          ═══════════          ═══════════
───────────          ───────────          ───────────
───────────          ───────────          ───────────
───────────          ───────────          ───────────
═══════════          ═══════════          ═══════════
```

Dynamic Range: Harmony:

Phrase Length: Texture:

Melody: Rhythm:

                             Form:

Other Comments:

SOLO MUSIC ANALYSIS

Instrument/voice classification _____

Title _____

Composer/Arranger _____

Publisher _____

Catalog Number _____   SELECTED   REJECTED

            DIFFICULT   MEDIUM   EASY

Range and tessitura (range notated in white notes; tessitura in black notes)

Text (for vocal solos):

Dynamic Range:

Phrase Length:

Rhythm:

Accompaniment:

Technical Problems (embellishments, articulation, embouchure, special effects, range, tessitura, fingerings, bowing, intonation, etc.):

Other Comments:

APPENDIX D

ELEMENTARY MUSIC MATERIALS AND MUSICAL INSTRUMENTS ANALYSIS CARD FORMS

ELEMENTARY MATERIALS ANALYSIS

Title _____

Author _____

Publisher _____ Date _____

Grade Level _____ Price _____

Format (book, records, pamphlets, series) _____
_____

Comments on art work, recordings, songs, supplementary material, etc.
_____
_____
_____

Comments on type of children these materials might appeal to (ethnic, regional, social, cultural, intellectual level) _____
_____
_____

How can materials be used with special education classes or handicapped children? _____
_____
_____

How much work with instruments is there?
_____
_____
_____

Other Comments _____
_____

ELEMENTARY MUSICAL INSTRUMENT ANALYSIS

Instrument _____

Manufacturer _____

Grade Level _____ Price _____

Key _____ Materials made of _____

Availability of Parts _____ Expense of Parts _____

Will the instrument stand abuse? _____

Will it stay in tune? _____

Possible playing problems for children _____

_____

_____

_____

Storage problems _____

Maintenance _____

_____

Method books or music currently available? _____

_____

Overall reaction _____

_____

_____

APPENDIX E

Pinpoint:

when? · *who?*

At the end of (class, lesson increment) the _____
will demonstrate acceptable

     student
     group
     class

What? · *How?*

_____ by _____

Examples:	Examples:
Performance ability	Playing the entire piece with-
sight-singing proficiency	out stopping
research of the classical	Sight-reading 8 measures with
period	80% accuracy
	Submitting a 20-page report
	free from factual error

Record:

(See above format)

At the beginning of the _____ the

_____ demonstrated _____

_____

by _____

_____

Consequate:

Time allotted for lesson or lesson increment: _____

    A. What you will do:

    B. How the student will respond
       (anticipation of successes and failures):

    C. Audio-visual aids (use at least two per lesson):

Evaluate:

    A. Students' successes and failures:

    B. Teacher's successes and failures:

APPENDIX F

INSTRUMENTAL LESSONS PROGRESS CHART

Name _____ Instrument _____

Lesson Schedule _____

Assignments	Lesson Dates									
1. Attendance										
2. Practice Time (Hrs. and Min.)										
3. Pages or Exercises completed in Methods Book										
4. Scales										
5. Arpeggios										
6. Sight-reading Rating										
7. Technical Ability Rating										
8. Rhythm Rating										
9. Knowledge of Musical Terms and Concepts										
10. Solos										
11. Intonation										
12. Interpretation										
13. Tone Quality										

Solos in Progress   Methods Books in Progress
        *indicates completed solos and methods books

_____   _____

_____   _____

_____   _____

Use other side for comments.

VOCAL LESSONS PROGRESS CHART

Name_____ Voice Range_____

Lesson Schedule_____

Assignments	Lesson Dates										
1. Attendance											
2. Practice Time (Hrs. and Min.)											
3. Diction											
4. Scales											
5. Vocalises											
6. Sight-reading Rating											
7. Technical Ability Rating											
8. Rhythm Rating											
9. Knowledge of Musical Terms and Concepts											
10. Solos											
11. Intonation											
12. Interpretation											
13. Tone Quality											

Solos in Progress   Vocalises in Progress
        *indicates completed solos and vocalises

_____   _____
_____   _____
_____   _____
_____   _____
_____   _____

Use other side for comments.

DAILY REHEARSAL PLAN

Pinpoint:

Record:

Warm-ups:

Sightreading:

Review of last rehearsal:

Consequate:

Evaluate:

APPENDIX H

PROFESSIONAL TIME LOG B

Name _____ Week Beginning _____ Ending _____

	MON.	TUES.	WED.	THURS.	FRI.	SAT.	SUN.	TOTAL HRS./MIN
A. OBSERVATION								
Teachers								
Students								
Other:								
B. LESSON PLANS/ASSIGN.								
Reading								
Writing								
Discussing								
Practicing								
Evaluation (correcting tests, etc.)								
C. CONVERSATIONS								
Students								
Teachers								
Administrators								
Others								
D. TEACHING								
Private Lessons								
Rehearsals (in school)								
Rehearsals (after school)								
Gen. Mus./Hist./Theory								
Elementary								
Other:								
E. CHANGING BEHAVIOR								
Observing/Recording								
Consequating								
Evaluation								
F. EXTRA-CURRICULAR DUTIES								
Bus Duty								
Hall Duty								
Meetings								
Lunch Duty								
Other:								

APPENDIX I

PERFORMANCE RATING FORM

#_____ Selection _____

Circle your rating:	Poor	Fair	Good	Excellent
Intonation	1	2	3	4
Blend	1	2	3	4
Balance	1	2	3	4
Tempo	1	2	3	4
Dynamics	1	2	3	4
Tone Quality	1	2	3	4
Rhythms	1	2	3	4
Phrasing	1	2	3	4
Ensemble	1	2	3	4
Diction	1	2	3	4
Style	1	2	3	4
Overall Artistic Effect . . . . (Musicality)	1	2	3	4
	___	___	___	___

Totals:

Rating_____

Rank_____

Judge's Name_____

APPENDIX J

MUSICAL EVALUATION

Teacher_____ Evaluator_____

(Rate each blank 1 through 10; 1 is low, 10 is high)

Did the teacher seem well-prepared and familiar with the
material used?   _____

Were the teacher's musical intentions clearly conveyed
through the presentation?   _____

Was the teacher able to identify and deal with important
musical problems? Rate items below that are either very good
or need improvement.

Intonation _____	Tone quality _____	Breathing _____	Consonants _____
Tempo _____	Vowels _____	Rhythm _____	Phrasing _____
Ensemble _____	Balance _____	Dynamics _____	Posture _____

Did the teacher achieve toward improvement of musicianship
and musical understanding?   _____

Did the teacher present creatively or attempt to stimulate student
creativity?   _____

What suggestions would you offer for the development of the
teacher's musical presentation?   _____

TEACHING EVALUATION

Teacher_____ Evaluator_____

(Rate each blank 1 through 10; 1 is low, 10 is high)

Did the teacher seem well-prepared and familiar with the
material used?   _____

Were the verbal instructions given by the teacher clear,
concise and easily heard?   _____

Did the teacher's approach to the group encourage you
to give your best efforts?   _____

Did the teacher present creatively or attempt to stimulate
student creativity?   _____

Did the teacher make effective use of teaching aids and
materials?   _____

How many times did the teacher approve/disapprove
student social and academic behavior?   Approve   _____

                                                             Disapprove _____

List four positive things the teacher did.

_____   _____

_____   _____

List one suggestion for improvement._____

142

APPENDIX K

ATTITUDE SURVEY FOR PERFORMANCE GROUPS

School_____ Name_____

Circle the number that best expresses your agreement or disagreement with each of the statements below:

Selection 1—

A. I like this *music*.

5	4	3	2	1
Strongly agree	Agree	Uncertain	Disagree	Strongly disagree

B. I enjoyed *rehearsing* this music.

5	4	3	2	1
Strongly agree	Agree	Uncertain	Disagree	Strongly disagree

C. I like this *conductor*.

5	4	3	2	1
Strongly agree	Agree	Uncertain	Disagree	Strongly disagree

D. During this rehearsal I was

5	4	3	2	1
Turned on	With it	Participating	Attending	Daydreaming

Selection 2—

A. I like this *music*.

5	4	3	2	1
Strongly agree	Agree	Uncertain	Disagree	Strongly disagree

B. I enjoyed *rehearsing* this music.

5	4	3	2	1
Strongly agree	Agree	Uncertain	Disagree	Strongly disagree

C. I like this *conductor*.

5	4	3	2	1
Strongly agree	Agree	Uncertain	Disagree	Strongly disagree

D. During this rehearsal I was

5	4	3	2	1
Turned on	With it	Participating	Attending	Daydreaming

ATTITUDE SURVEY FOR PRIMARY GRADES

The technique of circling either smiling, frowning, or neutral faces to represent varying degrees of preference may be used with very young children. By using one set of the following figures per item you can develop your own attitude survey.

For example, you might ask children to circle the face that represents how much they like to (1) go to school, (2) sing, (3) play the autoharp, and so forth.

APPENDIX M

ATTITUDE SURVEY FOR UPPER ELEMENTARY GRADES

We would like to find out how you feel about certain things in school. Please answer the following questions as honestly as you can. Circle the number to the left of the answer which best describes your feelings about each question. Thank you.

1. Did you like school this year?
   1. I almost never liked it.
   2. I didn't like it very much.
   3. I liked it sometimes.
   4. I liked it most of the time.
   5. I liked it almost all of the time.

2. Did you like your music class this year?
   1. I almost never liked it.
   2. I didn't like it very much.
   3. I liked it sometimes.
   4. I liked it most of the time.
   5. I liked it almost all of the time.

3. Do you wish you had music more often in school?
   1. Yes
   2. No

4. Did you like your music teacher this year?
   1. I almost never liked him/her.
   2. I didn't like him/her very much.
   3. I liked him/her sometimes.
   4. I liked him/her most of the time.
   5. I like him/her almost all of the time.

5. What would you say you did most of the time in music class this year?
   1. Sing
   2. Play instruments
   3. Listen to music
   4. Make up melodies
   5. Move or dance to music
   6. _____
   7. _____
   8. _____
   9. _____

6. What did you like to do most in music class?
   1. Play instruments
   2. Listen to music
   3. Sing
   4. Make up melodies
   5. Move or dance to music
   6. _____

7. What is your favorite instrument that you played in music class?
   1. _____
   2. _____
   3. _____
   4. _____
   5. _____
   6. _____

8. Do you have a record player in your home?
   1. Yes
   2. No

9. How often do you listen to music either on your record player or on the radio?
   1. Never
   2. Hardly ever
   3. Sometimes
   4. Often
   5. Very often

10. How often do your parents listen to music?
    1. Never
    2. Hardly ever
    3. Sometimes
    4. Often
    5. Very often

11. Did you like the concert played by the Columbus Orchestra?
    1. Not very much.
    2. Only a little.
    3. I enjoyed some of it.
    4. I enjoyed it.
    5. I enjoyed it very much.

12. What instrument did you play most often in music class?
    1. Mandolin
    2. Violin
    3. Autoharp
    4. Piano
    5. Guitar
    6. Bells
    7. Flutophone
    8. No response

13. What instrument did you like to play the best?

   1. _____
   2. _____
   3. _____
   4. _____
   5. _____
   6. _____
   7. _____
   8. _____

14. How often did you listen to music in music class this year?

   1. Never
   2. Not very often
   3. Sometimes
   4. Often
   5. Very often

15. Did you like the music you listened to in music class?

   1. Not any of it.
   2. Very little of it.
   3. Some of it.
   4. Most of it.
   5. Almost all of it.

16. How often did your class sing in music class this year?

   1. Never
   2. Not very often.
   3. Sometimes.
   4. Often.
   5. Very often.

17. Did you like singing in music class?

   1. Not at all.
   2. Not very much.
   3. Sometimes.
   4. Most of the time.
   5. Almost all of the time.

18. How much music would you like to have in school next year?

   1. None
   2. Less than we had this year.
   3. About the same as this year.
   4. A little more than this year.
   5. A lot more than this year.

19. Would you like to have the same music teacher next year?

   1. Yes   2. No

20. Did you ever make up melodies in music class this year?

   1. Never
   2. Hardly ever
   3. Sometimes
   4. Often
   5. Very often.

21. Did you ever make up rhythmic accompaniments in music class?

   1. Never   2. Hardly ever
   3. Sometimes   4. Often
        5. Very often

DIAGRAM AND EXPLANATION OF VIDEOTAPING PROCEDURES

Videotapes may be made using any standard videotape recorder, video camera, zoom lens, video monitor, lavalier microphone, microphone mixer, and cassette recorder.

The conductor's voice and the sound from the performing ensemble or class are recorded via the lavalier microphone. The microphone mixer mixes the sounds picked up on the lavalier microphone with sound ("observe-record" cues) from the cassette recorder. Sound can be monitored using a mini-earphone plugged into the video monitor.

The following is a diagram of the way the equipment should be set up:

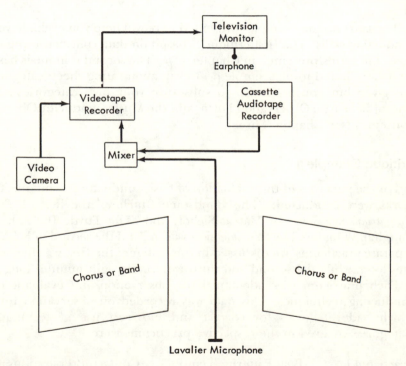

A Behavioral Observation cassette tape should be prerecorded before the videotaping session

APPENDIX O

CONDUCTING CRITIQUE EXAMPLES

The two critique examples presented here will help you evaluate your conducting skills. The first critique is based on data collected using observation forms presented in Chapter Five. The second critique is based on data collected using a simple peer evaluation rating sheet (categories are given but you may wish to substitute your own categories), the Choral Rehearsal Observation Form, and the Music Conductor Observation Form (see Chapter Three).

Critique Example 1

For the purposes of this evaluation of basic conducting technique, two works were conducted: "The Handsome Butcher," the first of *Three Hungarian Folk Songs* by Matyas Sieber, and "The Turtle Dove" by R. Vaughan Williams. The first selection was in $\frac{2}{4}$ and the second in $\frac{4}{4}$. Three separate practicums are discussed in this critique; the first was five minutes long, while the second and third were both eight minutes long.

Each practicum was videotaped for observation and evaluation of conducting techniques. This data was recorded on observation forms which had categories for correct and incorrect use of techniques. Categories covered in the respective practicums were:

Practicum I: Beat Patterns, Tempo, Eye Contact, Preparations and Releases
Practicum II: All categories in Practicum I, plus Dynamics and Cueing
Practicum III: All categories in Practicum II, plus Style.

Data was collected in accordance with "observe" and "record" intervals, which were given verbally on the videotape. In addition to myself, the videotape was viewed by a reliability observer. Reliability was calculated by dividing the number of agreements by the total number of agreements plus disagreements. The resulting number represented the percentage of agreement between myself and the reliability observer. Reliabilities for the three practicums were as follows:

Practicum I   79% Agreement
Practicum II   96% Agreement
Practicum III   83% Agreement

The following table contains the percentage of correct responses for each category for each practicum:

Table 1 Percentages of Correct Responses in Practicums

	Percentages Correct		
Categories	*Practicum I*	*Practicum II*	*Practicum III*
Beat Patterns	45%	62%	82%
Tempo	33%	78%	82%
Eye Contact	28%	38%	70%
Preparations	47%	84%	92%
Releases	50%	73%	75%
Dynamics	*n.o.	81%	96%
Cueing	n.o.	92%	98%
Style	n.o.	n.o.	93%

*n.o. = not observed for that practicum.

The following section includes a discussion of strengths and weaknesses within each of the conducting technique categories observed and evaluated:

Beat Pattern and Tempo

It is obvious after viewing the videotape, that there are numerous areas of my conducting that need improvement. One of the primary weaknesses is in the area of beat pattern and tempo. In all three practicums, maintaining a steady beat pattern has been a problem. There were times when an entire beat or more would be dropped and it was difficult to keep things going. This may have been due to a lack of independence of hands, especially in the first practicum. This problem can be overcome by practicing the beat patterns by themselves with no attention being given to the other conducting competencies and by concentration on restricting unnecessary body movement.

The beat pattern problem also creates problems with variances in tempo. Tempos became fairly accurate by practicum III, though at times uncalled-for ritardandos were apparent. Again, increased practice time will best help to eliminate this deficiency.

Eye Contact

In the first practicum my eyes were glued to the score. By the third practicum I had my head up and out of the score, but then my eyes were closed part of the time. Complete score memorization and practice in front of a mirror should help solve this problem.

Preparations and Releases

Preparations were fairly effective but a standard must be achieved whereby a given motion will always convey the desired tempo, dynamic, mood, etc. My releases were often aimlessly done, being in a hurry to restart the piece. I must consciously think of the release as being equally important to the preparation.

Body movement and gesture were generally used in preparations, releases and cues, but need to be made with more authority. More than anything, I think that increased performance time and, as a result, a higher level of confidence will be the most valuable aids in effectively improving body movement and gesture.

Dynamics and Style

I have a problem with style. There is a tendency to get carried away with creating an affective response at times, and basic conducting techniques begin to suffer. Excessive motion in beat patterns and body movement should be avoided.

The biggest problem with dynamics was the beat pattern not being the appropriate size to indicate the desired dynamic level. Also, left hand indications were not definitive enough.

Cueing

In a sense, cueing may have been my best category in that it was usually not incorrect. However, eye contact should be established sooner before each cue to promote more accurate entrances.

In conclusion, I encountered no problems with the operational definitions. On the contrary, I found them quite sufficient for establishing a foundation for basic conducting technique when followed up with some of the suggested supplementary readings.

Critique Example 2

In order to evaluate my conducting objectively, several techniques were used to collect data. Each evaluator filled out a Conductor Evaluation Form. On this form, they were asked to rate me in eleven categories on a scale of 1 (poor) to 5 (excellent). These eleven categories were:

1. Beat Clarity and Precision
2. Style Gesture
3. Starts and Stops
4. Beat Note Choice
5. Tempo
6. Entrance Cueing
7. Interpretation
8. Dynamics
9. Score Preparation
10. Rehearsal Procedure
11. Leadership

Two of my rehearsals were recorded on videotape and I viewed the videotapes several days after the actual rehearsals, using the Choral Rehearsal Observation Form and the Music Conductor Observation Form. The former facilitates observation of student activity, student on/off-task, and teacher response. However, in these rehearsals no student observation was made. The only student activity observed was performance activity. Teacher activities observed included instruction, singing, and reinforcement. The Music Conductor Observation Form is used to objectively observe Activity—instruction, singing during group performance, teaching during group performance; Body Movement—approach, departure, stationary; Conducting Gestures—strict, expressive, none; Eye Contact—group, individual, music, other; Facial Expressions—approving, disapproving, neutral; Speech Speed—steady, hesitant, repetitive; Voice Pitch—low, variable, high; Voice Volume—soft, normal, loud. It can also be used to record any mannerisms and their frequency.

The data collected from Conductor Evaluation Forms, Choral Rehearsal Observation Forms, and Music Conductor Observation Forms is presented here in Appendix Tables 2 through 5. Appendix Table 6 shows competency levels which I set and my ability to achieve them.

Table 2 Average Ratings Conductor Evaluation Forms

Categories	First Rehearsal	Second Rehearsal
Beat Clarity and Precision	3.39	4.00
Style Gesture	3.24	2.78
Starts and Stops	3.26	3.26
Beat Note Choice	3.47	4.00
Tempo	3.53	4.22
Entrance Cueing	3.32	3.32
Interpretation	3.95	4.22
Dynamics	3.79	3.61
Score Preparation	4.16	4.42
Rehearsal Procedure	3.74	4.56
Leadership	3.71	4.42
TOTAL OVERALL RATING	3.60	4.07

Table 3 Use of Rehearsal Time in Minutes

Behavior	First Rehearsal	Second Rehearsal
Performance (Entire Group)	3.75	4.00
Sectionals	.50	.25
Instruction	3.25	3.75
Other	.50	.00

Table 4 Percentage of Nonverbal Behavior

Behavior	First Rehearsal	Second Rehearsal
Body Movement	0	30
Strict Conducting	47	26
Expressive Conducting	53	74
Eye Contact	76	94
Approval Facial Expression	9	13
Disapproval Facial Expression	9	0

Table 5 Frequency of Verbal Behavior

Behavior	First Rehearsal	Second Rehearsal
Singing during Performance	0	0
Teaching during Performance	2	8
Approvals	2	7
Disapprovals	4	0
Reinforcement Errors	0	0
Steady Speaking	13	14
Hesitant Speaking	10	11
Repetitive Speaking	0	0
Low Voice Pitch	13	4
High Voice Pitch	0	0
Variable Voice Pitch	7	21
Soft Volume	2	0
Normal Volume	17	21
Loud Volume	1	4

Table 6 Competencies: Percentages Set and Achieved

Competency Category	Level Set	Levels Achieved	
		First Rehearsal	Second Rehearsal
Eye Contact	80	76	94
Expressive Conducting	65	53	74

This data gives much information which I can use in improving my conducting. There are several categories which I am particularly anxious to improve. In others, I was very happy to find improvement from the first rehearsal to the second.

The overall improvement in the ratings on the Conductor Evaluation Form was from 3.6 to 4.07. Greatest improvement was in the categories of Rehearsal Procedure (from 3.74 to 4.56) and Tempo (from 3.53 to 4.22). I feel that my improved rehearsal procedure was based on feeling more comfortable with the music and dealing more with musical aspects than with technical ones. I am not really interested in my improvement in Tempo.

Group opinion is much more important in categories such as Beat Clarity and Precision (ratings improved from 3.39 to 4.00), Starts and Stops (ratings remained the same), Entrance Cueing (ratings remained the same), and Leadership (ratings improved from 3.71 to 4.42). The first three are categories in which a good conductor is vital to the group's ability to follow directions. The fourth is, I feel, equally important, for a conductor who does not show leadership qualities will be unable to develop rapport with or the respect of the group over a long period of time. I was generally happy with these figures except for that in Cueing. I definitely need to practice cueing, and I want to show improvement in this skill in the near future.

Basically, I think it is good to know what others think about my conducting in certain categories. If they have trouble understanding my instructions or following my beat pattern or conducting gestures, I would want to know this. I have become increasingly aware of the discrepancy between the way I perceive my behavior and the way others perceive it.

The aspect of my conducting which I would most like to improve is that of speech speed. During the first rehearsal 43% of my speech was hesitant; during the second rehearsal, this figure was 44%. Ideally it should be reduced to 0%. I feel that this problem may be reduced through the use of a highly detailed rehearsal plan and a good deal of thinking ahead about what I am going to say.

Other aspects of my speech also need improvement. I need to change my tone of voice so that my approvals are less "sing-song." My approval repertory is rather limited: all of my seven approvals during the second rehearsal were "good" or "very good." I would like all of my reinforcers to be different so that they do not lose their effectiveness. It would also be helpful if my voice volume were more variable, particularly if I raised my voice and were more enthusiastic in my approvals.

Nonverbal behaviors were for the most part better than verbal ones. I improved in almost every category including those in which I set competencies. However, my facial expressions were more neutral during the second rehearsal than they were during the first rehearsal. I need to work on this in the future.

During both of my conducting presentations, I was aware of the large amount of time I spent instructing. I feel that 47% of the rehearsal is, as a rule, too much time to spend on nonperformance activities. One way I could reduce this figure would be, again, to plan my words carefully, to say what needs to be said, and to get going again. In a first rehearsal of a piece, probably two-thirds of the rehearsal should be spent in performance activities. As the group becomes more proficient with the music, this should be increased to a maximum level.

Both of the competency levels which were established before the first rehearsal were met and surpassed. In the future, I will not concentrate on these two areas, although I will not ignore them. I would like to see myself achieving a four-to-one ratio of approvals to disapprovals and to expand my approval repertory in the next few months. I would also like to eliminate hesitant speaking. These are the two areas in which I will put the most emphasis during student teaching.

APPENDIX P

WEEKLY MUSIC TEACHING EVALUATION

TEACHER_____ DATE_____ SCHOOL_____

EVALUATOR_____

PERSONALITY

	Very Much		Average		Not at All
Aggressive					
Enthusiastic or optimistic					
Critical					
Sarcastic					
Reliable					
Punctual					
Cooperative					
Confident					
Timid, Shy					
Pessimistic					
Apathetic					
Tactful					
Antagonistic					

MUSICAL

	Weak 1	2	3	4	Strong 5
Knowledge of subject matter					
Knowledge of instruments or voice					
Teaching skills					
Enthusiasm for teaching					
Ability to Communicate: Verbal					
Musical					
Organizational ability					
Conducting ability					
Ability to maintain discipline					
Ability to adapt to various grade levels					
Desire for improvement or potential					
Initiative					
Leadership					
Planning					
Ability to motivate					

EVALUATOR'S SIGNATURE_____

TEACHER'S SIGNATURE_____

APPENDIX Q

EVALUATION OF MUSIC INSTRUCTION

Teacher being evaluated _____ Date _____

Course _____

	low			high	does not apply

1. The instructor demonstrates broad, accurate and up-to-date knowledge of subject matter (including music literature).   1 2 3 4 5 0

2. The instructor relates the material of this course to other fields and to present day problems.   1 2 3 4 5 0

3. The instructor is honest in admitting mistakes and/or lack of sufficient knowledge.   1 2 3 4 5 0

4. Course objectives and/or assignments are reasonable in regard to time available, materials available, and student abilities.   1 2 3 4 5 0

5. The instructor deals with information and/or skills which you believe important to professional training or to life in general.   1 2 3 4 5 0

6. How well organized is this instructor? How well do course objectives agree with the material covered in class?   1 2 3 4 5 0

7. How efficient is the instructor in the use of class (private lesson, rehearsal) time?   1 2 3 4 5 0

8. How often is the instructor present and on time for class (private lesson, rehearsal)?   1 2 3 4 5 0

9. From your point of view, how adequately is instructional material covered?   1 2 3 4 5 0

10. How helpful is the textbook and/or other required material in learning the subject matter?   1 2 3 4 5 0

11. How helpful are grade producing situations in gaining comprehension of course material?   1 2 3 4 5 0

12. How fair and impartial are grade producing situations?   1 2 3 4 5 0

13. Does the instructor welcome differences of opinion?   1   2   3   4   5   0

14. Are the explanations of the instructor clear and understandable?   1   2   3   4   5   0

15. How effectively does the instructor use instructional aids (handouts, programmed instruction, audio-visual equipment, charts, etc.) to explain and clarify the content of this course?   1   2   3   4   5   0

16. How would you rate this instructor's sense of humor? (e.g., did the instructor enjoy humor, yet know when to be serious?)   1   2   3   4   5   0

17. How effective is the instructor in motivating students to do sound, independent thinking, and/or independent work outside of class?   1   2   3   4   5   0

18. How friendly and willing is the instructor in helping students outside of class?   1   2   3   4   5   0

19. In comparison with other university instructors you have had, do you rate this instructor as being in the   1   2   3   4   5   0
            (1) bottom 10%
            (2) bottom 30%
            (3) average
            (4) top 30%
            (5) top 10%

20, 21, 22, and 23 are applicable to applied music courses (private lessons, method classes, and ensembles) only.

20. To what degree do you agree with the instructor's interpretation of music literature?   1   2   3   4   5   0

21. How well does the instructor demonstrate that knowledge of technical problems of playing and/or singing is broad, accurate, and up-to-date? If this course is an ensemble, consider the instructor's knowledge of rehearsal techniques.   1   2   3   4   5   0

22. When conducting (if applicable), how effective are the gestures of the instructor in conveying what the instructor desires in regard to performing the music?   1   2   3   4   5   0

23. How effective is the instructor in helping students with "stage fright" problems?   1   2   3   4   5   0

24. How much do you feel you have learned   1   2   3   4   5   0
    (improved applied performance) during
    this instructional period?   no   yes

25. Does the instructor test in any way to   1   2
    determine if students have prerequisite
    knowledge and skills for taking this course?

26. Is the instructor's speech clear and distinct?   1   2

27. Is the instructor's manner pleasing and free   1   2
    from annoying mannerisms? [If not, specify
    the annoying mannerism(s).]

    _____

    _____

    _____

28. Is a course syllabus provided?   1   2

29. On which of the following do you think the   1   2   3   4   5   0
    instructor based grades?
            (1) natural ability
            (2) achievement of clearly
                defined objectives
            (3) attendance
            (4) other (specify)_____

    _____
            (5) don't know

30. Which of the following statements characterizes   1   2   3
    this instructor's interaction?
            (1) Praises his students most of the
                time.
            (2) Criticizes his students most of
                the time.
            (3) Praises and criticizes his students
                fairly and impartially in accordance
                with their achievement.

31. How many times within the current academic year   _____
    did you observe this instructor? (Students list
    contact hours per week; faculty list number of
    observations.)

32. How many times within the current academic year   _____
    have you received inferential knowledge of this   _____
    instructor's teaching effectiveness from his/her   _____
            (1) students' verbal reports   _____
            (2) students' musical performance
            (3) instructors' musical performance
            (4) professional colleagues

33. What things did you dislike about this course and/or this instructor?

34. What things did you *like* about this course and/or this instructor?

IN THE FOLLOWING SPACES, THE INSTRUCTOR MAY INSERT
ADDITIONAL TEST ITEMS:

35.

36.

37.

Bibliography

ABELES, H. F., "Student Perceptions of Characteristics of Effective Applied Music Instructors," *Journal of Research in Music Education* 23 (Summer 1975): 147–54.

ALLEY, JAYNE M., "Competency Based Evaluation of a Music Therapy Curriculum," *Journal of Music Therapy* XV (Spring 1978): 9–14.

ALTMAN, K. I., and T. E. LINTON, "Operant Conditioning in the Classroom Setting: A Review of the Research," *Journal of Educational Research* 64 (1971): 277–86.

ASCARE, DONALD, and SAUL AXELROD, "Use of a Behavior Modification Procedure Four 'Open' Classrooms," *Psychology in the Schools* X (April 1973): 243–48.

AYLLON, TEODORO, and MICHAEL D. ROBERTS, "Eliminating Discipline Problems by Strengthening Academic Performance," *Journal of Applied Behavior Analysis* 7 (Spring 1974): 71–76.

BAER, ANN M., TRUDYLEE ROWBURY, and DONALD M. BAER, "The Development of Instructional Control over Classroom Activities of Deviant Pre-School Children," *Journal of Applied Behavior Analysis* 6 (Summer 1973): 289–98.

BANDURA, ALBERT, *Principles of Behavior Modification,* New York: Holt, Rinehart and Winston, 1969.

———, "Vicarious Processes: A Case of No-Trial Learning," in *Advances in Experimental Social Psychology,* ed. Leonard Berkowitz, vol. 2, pp. 1–55. New York: Academic Press, 1965.

BANDURA, ALBERT, and RICHARD H. WALTERS, *Social Learning and Personality Development.* New York: Holt, Rinehart and Winston, 1963.

BECKER, WESLEY C., SIEGFRIED ENGLEMANN, and DON R. THOMAS, *Teaching: A Course in Applied Psychology,* Chicago: Science Research Associates, 1971.

BECKER, WESLEY C., CHARLES H. MADSEN, JR., CAROLE REVELLE ARNOLD, and DON R. THOMAS, "The Contingent Use of Teacher Attention and Praise in Reducing Classroom Behavior Problems," *Journal of Special Education* 1 (1967): 287–307.

BONEY, JOAN, and LOIS RHEA, *A Guide to Student Teaching in Musia*. Englewood Cliffs, N.J.: Prentice-Hall, 1970.

BOYLE, DAVID, and KEITH P. THOMPSON, "Changing Inservice Teachers' Self-Perceptions of Their Ability to be Effective Teachers of the Arts," *Journal of Research in Music Education* 24 (Winter 1976): 187–96.

BRAND, MANNY, "Effectiveness of Simulation Techniques in Teaching Behavior Management," *Journal of Research in Music Education* 25 (Summer 1977): 131–38.

BREYER, NORMAN L., and GEORGE J. ALLEN, "Effects of Implementing a Token Economy on Teacher Attending Behavior," *Journal of Applied Behavior Analysis* 8 (Winter 1975): 373–80.

BRODEN, MARCIA, GLENNA COPELAND, ALVA BEASLEY, and R. VANCE HALL, "Altering Student Responses Through Changes in Teacher Verbal Behavior," *Journal of Applied Behavior Analysis* 10 (Fall 1977): 479–87.

BROWN, AMY, "Effects of Televised Instruction on Student Music Selection, Music Skills, and Attitudes," *Journal of Research in Music Education* 26 (Winter 1978): 445–55.

BROWN, DAVID, DANIEL RESCHLY, and HOWARD WASSERMAN, "Effects of Surreptitious Modeling upon Teacher Classroom Behaviors," *Psychology in the Schools* XI (1974(: 366–69.

BUFFORD, RODGER K., "Evaluation of a Reinforcement Procedure for Accelerating Work Rate in a Self-Paced Course," *Journal of Applied Behavior Analysis* 9 (Summer 1976): 208. Abstract.

CADY, HENRY L., "Seeking a Theory for Music Education," *Music Educators Journal* 65 (May 1979): 34–37.

CARLSEN, JAMES C., *Melodic Perception*. New York: McGraw-Hill, 1975.

CARNINE, DOUGLAS W., "Effects of Two Teacher-Presentation Rates on Off-Task Behavior, Answering Correctly and Participation," *Journal of Applied Behavior Analysis* 9 (Summer 1976): 199–206.

COLWELL, RICHARD, *The Evaluation of Music Teaching and Learning*. Englewood Cliffs, N.J.: Prentice-Hall, 1970.

———, *The Teaching of Instrumental Music*. New York: Meredith Corp., 1969.

COSSAIRT, ACE, R. VANCE HALL, and B. L. HOPKINS, "The Effects of Experimenter's Instructions, Feedback and Praise on Teacher Praise and Student Attending Behavior," *Journal of Applied Behavior Analysis* 6 (Spring 1973): 89–100.

DARCH, CRAIG B., and HAROLD W. THORPE, "The Principal Game: A Group Consequence Procedure to Increase Classroom On-Task Behavior," *Psychology in the Schools* XIV (1977): 341–47.

DIETZ, SAMUEL M., and ALAN C. REPP, "Decreasing Classroom Misbehavior Through the Use of DRL Schedules of Reinforcement," *Journal of Applied Behavior Analysis* 6 (Fall 1973): 457–63.

————, "Differentially Reinforcing Low Rates of Misbehavior with Normal Elementary School Children," *Journal of Applied Behavior Analysis* 7 (Winter 1974): 622. Abstract.

DORMAN, PHYLLIS E., "Relationship Between Teaching Incidents and Taba's Theoretical Construct," *Journal of Research in Music Education* 21 (Summer 1973): 182–86.

DOROW, LAURA, G., "The Effect of Teacher Approval/Disapproval Ratios on Student Music Selection and Concert Attentiveness," *Journal of Research in Music Education* 25 (Spring 1977): 32–40.

DOROW, LAURA G., and R. DOUGLAS GREER, "The Reinforcement Value of a Music Instrument for Beginning Instrumentalists and the Influence of Discovery Versus Teacher Approval on Achievement," *Journal of Music Therapy* XIV (Spring 1977): 2–16.

DRABMAN, RONALD, ROBERT SPITALNIK, and KAREN SPITALNIK, "Sociometric and Disruptive Behavior as a Function of Four Types of Token Reinforcement Programs," *Journal of Applied Behavior Analysis* 7 (Spring 1974): 93–101.

DuNANN, DEBORAH H., and STEPHEN J. WEBER, "Short- and Long-Term Effects of Contingency-Managed Instruction on Low, Medium and High G.P.A. Students," *Journal of Applied Behavior Analysis* 9 (Fall 1976): 375. Abstract.

EICKMANN, PAUL E., and RONALD T. LEE, "Applying an Instructional Development Process to Music Education," *Council for Research in Music Education* (Winter 1977): 1–22.

ELLIOTT, CHARLES A., "Attacks and Releases as Factors in Instrument Identification," *Journal of Research in Music Education* 23 (Spring 1975): 35–40.

ENGLEMANN, SIEGFRIED, "The Effectiveness of Direct Verbal Instruction on I.Q. Performance and Achievement in Reading and Arithmetic," in *An Empirical Basis for Change in Education,* ed. Wesley C. Becker, pp. 461–83. Chicago: Science Research Associates, 1971.

ERBES, ROBERT L., and CHARLES HICKS, "The Implementation of the Rehearsal Interaction Observation System in a Teacher Training Program." Paper read at the Music Educators National Conference, March 1976, Atlantic City, New Jersey.

ERNST ROY E., *Developing Competencies in Teaching Instrumental Music.* Fairport, N.Y.: ERGO Publications, 1979.

ERNST, ROY E., and MILFORD FARGO, *Developing Competencies in Teaching Vocal and General Music,* Fairport, N.Y.: ERGO Publications, 1979.

FELIXBROD, JEFFREY J., and K. DANIEL O'LEARY, "Effects of Reinforcement on Children's Academic Behavior as a Function of Self-Determined and Externally Imposed Contingencies," *Journal of Applied Behavior Analysis* 6 (Summer 1973): 241–50.

FISKE, HAROLD E., JR., "Judge-Group Differences in the Rating of Secondary School Trumpet Performances," *Journal of Research in Music Education* 23 (Fall 1975): 186–96.

FORSYTHE, JERE L., "The Effect of Teacher Approval, Disapproval, and Errors on Student Attentiveness: Music versus Classroom Teachers," in *Research in Music Behavior,* ed. Clifford K. Madsen, R. Douglas Greer, and Charles H. Madsen, Jr., pp. 49–55. New York: Teachers College Press, Columbia University, 1975.

———, "Elementary Student Attending Behavior as a Function of Classroom Activities," *Journal of Research in Music Education* 25 (Fall 1977): 228–39.

FROEHLICH, HILDEGARD, "Replication of a Study on Teaching Singing in the Elementary General Music Classroom," *Journal of Research in Music Education* 27 (Spring 1979): 35–45.

GERINGER, JOHN M., "An Assessment of Children's Musical Instrument Preferences," *Journal of Music Therapy* XIV (Winter 1977): 172–79.

GLYNN, E. L., and J. D. THOMAS, "Effect of Cueing on Self-Control of Classroom Behavior," *Journal of Applied Behavior Analysis* 7 (Summer 1974): 299–306.

GLYNN, E. L., J. D. THOMAS, and SEOK M. SHEE, "Behavioral Self-Control of On-Task Behavior in an Elementary Classroom," *Journal of Applied Behavior Analysis* 6 (Spring 1973): 105–13

GONZO, CARROLL, "Aesthetic Experiences: A Coming of Age in Music Education," *Music Educators Journal* 58 (December, 1971): 34.

GONZO, CARROLL, and JERE FORSYTHE, "Developing and Using Videotapes to Teach Rehearsal Techniques and Principles," *Journal of Research in Music Education* 24 (Spring 1976): 32–41.

GORDON, EDWIN, *The Psychology of Music Teaching*. Englewood Cliffs, N.J.: Prentice-Hall, 1971.

GRAHAM, RICHARD M., ed., *Music for the Exceptional Child*. Reston, Virginia: Music Educators National Conference, 1975.

GRANDY, GORDON, CHARLES H. MADSEN, JR., and LOIS M. DE MERSSEMAN, "The Effects of Individual and Interdependent Contingencies on Inappropriate Classroom Behavior," *Psychology in the Schools* X (1973): 488–93.

GREEN, ELIZABETH A. H., *The Modern Conductor*. Englewood Cliffs, N.J.: Prentice-Hall, 1969.

GREENBERG, MARVIN, "Research in Early Childhood Education: A Survey with Recommendations," *Council for Research in Music Education,* no. 45 (1976): 1–20.

GREENFIELD, DIANNE G., "Evaluation of Music Therapy Practicum Competencies: Comparisons of Self- and Instructor Ratings of Videotapes," *Journal of Music Therapy* XV (Spring 1978): 15–20.

GREENWOOD, CHARLES R., HYMAN HOPS, JOSEPH DELQUADRI, and JACQUELINE GUILD, "Group Contingencies for Group Consequences in Classroom Management: A Further Analysis," *Journal of Applied Behavior Analysis* 7 (Fall 1974): 413–25.

GREENWOOD, CHARLES R., HOWARD N. SLOANE, JR., and ARLENE BASKIN, "Training Elementary Aged Peer-Behavior Managers to Control Small Group Programmed Mathematics," *Journal of Applied Behavior Analysis* 7 (Spring 1974): 103–14.

GREER, R. DOUGLAS, LAURA G. DOROW, and ANDREW RANDALL, "Music Listening Preferences of Elementary School Children," *Journal of Research in Music Education* 22 (Winter 1974): 284–91.

GREER, R. DOUGLAS, LAURA G. DOROW, GUSTAV WACHHAUS, and ELMER R. WHITE, "Adult Approval and Students' Music Selection Behavior," *Journal of Research in Music Education* 21 (Winter 1973): 345–54.

GREER, R. DOUGLAS, ANDREW RANDALL, and CRAIG TIMBERLAKE, "The Discriminate Use of Music Listening as a Contingency for Improvement in Vocal Pitch Acuity and Attending Behavior," *Council for Research in Music Education,* no. 26 (1971): 10–18.

HAIR, HARRIET I., "Discrimination of Tonal Direction on Verbal and Nonverbal Tasks by First Grade Children," *Journal of Research in Music Education* 25 (Fall 1977): 197–210.

HALL, R. VANCE, DIANE LUND, and DELORIS JACKSON, "Effects of Teacher Attention on Study Behavior," *Journal of Applied Behavior Analysis* 1 (1968): 1–12.

HANLEY, EDWARD M., "Review of Research Involving Applied Behavior Analysis in the Classroom," *Review of Educational Research* 40 (1970): 597–625.

HARRIS, V. WILLIAM, and JAMES A. SHERMAN, "Effects of Peer Tutoring and Consequences on the Math Performance of Elementary Classroom Students," *Journal of Applied Behavior Analysis* 6 (Winter 1973): 587–97.

———, "Homework, Assignments, Consequences, and Classroom Performance in Social Studies and Mathematics," *Journal of Applied Behavior Analysis* 7 (Winter 1974): 505–19.

———, "Use and Analysis of the 'Good Behavior Game' to Reduce Disruptive Classroom Behavior," *Journal of Applied Behavior Analysis* 6 (Fall 1973): 405–417.

HAYES, LOUISE A., "The Use of Group Contingencies for Behavioral Control: A Review," *Psychological Bulletin* 83 (1976): 628–48.

HEDDEN, STEVEN K., "Meaning of the Concept of Music Teacher to High School Musicians," *Journal of Research in Music Education* 21 (Winter 1973): 366–71.

HODGES, DONALD A., "A New Way to Start the Day (Warm-Up Exercises)," *The Instrumentalist* 31 (March 1977): 98–99.

HOFFER, CHARLES R., "Teaching Useful Knowledge in Rehearsal," *Music Educators Journal* 52 (January 1966): 49–51, 90–94.

HOLT, DENNIS M., "Competency-Based Music Teacher Education: Is Systematic Accountability Worth the Effort?" *Council for Research in Music Education* (Winter 1974): 1–6.

HORTON, GARY O., "Generalization of Teacher Behavior as a Function of Subject Matter Specific Discriminative Training," *Journal of Applied Behavior Analysis* 8 (Fall 1975): 311–19.

HOUSTON, W. ROBERT, ed., *Exploring Competency-Based Education*. Berkeley, Calif.: McCutchan Publishing Corp., 1974.

HOUSTON, W. ROBERT, and ROBERT B. HOWSAM, eds., *Competency-Based Teacher Education: Progress, Problems, and Prospects*. Chicago: Science Research Associates, Inc., 1972.

HUGHES, WILLIAM O., *A Concise Introduction to Teaching Elementary School Music*. Belmont, California: Wadsworth Publishing Co., 1973.

HUNDERT, JOEL, BRADLEY BUCHER, and MICHAEL HENDERSON, "Increasing Appropriate Classroom Behaviour and Academic Performance by Reinforcing Correct Work Alone," *Psychology in the Schools* XIII (1976): 195–200.

JELLISON, JUDITH A., and MARY L. HELGESEN, "Music in the Education of Exceptional Children: Teacher Competencies," Minneapolis, Minnesota: University of Minnesota, Dean's Grant Project, 1978.

JETTER, JUNE THOMSEN, "An Instructional Model for Teaching Identification and Naming of Music Phenomena to Preschool Children," *Journal of Research in Music Education* 26 (Summer 1978): 97–110.

JOHNSON, MARTHA, and JON S. BAILEY, "Cross-Age Tutoring: Fifth Graders as Arithmetic Tutors for Kindergarten Children," *Journal of Applied Behavior Analysis* 7 (Summer 1974): 223–32.

KAUFFMAN, JAMES M., JUDITH L. NUSSEN, and CHARLES S. McGEE, "Follow-up in Classroom Behavior Modification: Survey and Discussion," *Journal of School Psychology* 15 (1977): 343–48.

KAZDIN, ALAN E., "The Effect of Vicarious Reinforcement on Attentive Behavior in the Classroom," *Journal of Applied Behavior Analysis* 6 (Spring 1973): 71–78.

KAZDIN, ALAN E., and JOAN KLOCK, "The Effect of Non-Verbal Teacher Approval on Student Attentive Behavior," *Journal of Applied Behavior Analysis* 6 (Winter 1973): 643–54.

KAZDIN, ALAN E., NANCY A. SILVERMAN, and JUDITH L. SITTLER, "The Use of Prompts to Enhance Vicarious Effects of Non-Verbal Approval," *Journal of Applied Behavior Analysis* 8 (Fall 1975): 279–86.

KELLER, FRED S., and EMILIO RIBES-INESTA, eds., *Behavior Modification: Applications to Education*. New York: Academic Press, 1974.

KENNEDY, WALLACE A., and HERMAN C. WILLCUTT, "Praise and Blame as Incentives," *Psychological Bulletin* 62 (1964): 323–32.

KIRK, COLLEEN J., "Preparing the Next Generation of Choral Conductors," *Choral Journal* XVIV (October 1978): 12–16.

KLEMISH, JANICE J., "A Comparative Study of Two Methods of Teaching Music Reading to First-Grade Children," *Journal of Research in Music Education* 18 (1970): 355–64.

KNAPCZYK, DENNIS R., and GARY LIVINGSTON, "The Effects of Prompting Question-Asking upon On-Task Behavior and Reading Comprehension," *Journal of Applied Behavior Analysis* 7 (Spring 1974): 115–21.

Koch, Larry, and Norman L. Breyer, "A Token Economy for the Teacher," *Psychology in the Schools* XI (1974): 195–200.

Kuhn, Terry Lee, "The Effect of Teacher Approval and Disapproval on Attentiveness, Musical Achievement, and Attitude of Fifth-Grade Students," in *Research in Music Behavior*, eds. Clifford K. Madsen, R. Douglas Greer, and Charles H. Madsen, Jr., pp. 40–48. New York: Teachers College Press, Columbia University, 1975.

Kuhn, Wolfgang, "Microteaching," *Music Educators Journal* 55 (December 1968): 49–53.

Labuta, Joseph A., *Guide to Accountability in Music Education*. West Nyack, N.Y.: Parker Publishing Company, Inc., 1974.

LeBlanc, Albert, "An Exploration of Fifth Grade Students' Musical Taste," Paper read at Symposium on Research in Music Behavior, November 1978, Atlanta, Georgia.

Lee, Portia, "The Effect of Approval Mistakes of Reinforcement on Classroom Behavior," Unpublished Master's thesis, Florida State University, 1975.

Lee, Ronald T., "The Competency-Based Music Education Curriculum: A Solution or Problem." *The American Music Teacher* (February/March 1977): 16–18.

Lehman, Paul R., *Tests and Measurements in Music*. Englewood Cliffs, N.J.: Prentice-Hall, 1968.

Leonhard, Charles, and Richard J. Colwell, "Research in Music Education," *Council for Research in Music Education* (Winter 1976): 1–30.

Levenkron, Jeffrey, David A. Santogrossi, and K. Daniel O'Leary, "Increasing Academic Performance Through Contingent Access to Tutoring," *Psychology in the Schools* XI (1974): 201–7.

Libb, J. Wesley, Carol Sachs, and William Boyd, "Reinforcement Strategies for Token Economies in a Special Classroom Setting," *Psychological Reports* 32 (1973): 831–34.

Lipe, Dewey, and Steven M. Jung, "Manipulating Incentives to Enhance School Learning," *Review of Educational Research* 41 (1971): 249–80.

Litow, Leon, and Donald K. Pumroy, "A Brief Review of Classroom Group-Oriented Contingencies," *Journal of Applied Behavior Analysis* 8 (Fall 1975): 341–47.

Long, James D., and Robert L. Williams, "The Comparative Effectiveness of Group and Individually Contingent Free Time with Inner-City Junior High School Students," *Journal of Applied Behavior Analysis* 6 (Fall 1973): 465–74.

McCarty, Timothy, Susan Griffin, Tony Apolloni, and Richard E. Shores, "Increased Peer-Teaching with Group-Oriented Contingencies for Arithmetic Performance in Behavior-Disordered Adolescents," *Journal of Applied Behavior Analysis* 10 (Summer 1977): 313. Abstract.

McElheran, Brock, *Conducting Techniques*. New York: Oxford University Press, 1966.

McLaughlin, T. F., "The Applicability of Token Reinforcement Systems in Public School Systems," *Psychology in the Schools* XII (1975): 84–89.

————, "A Review of Applications of Group-Contingency Procedures Used in Behavior Modification in the Regular Classroom: Some Recommendations for School Personnel," *Psychological Reports* 35 (1974): 1299–1303.

McLaughlin, Thomas F., and J. E. Malaby, "The Utilization of an Individual Contingency Program to Control Assignment Completion in a Token Classroom: A Case Study," *Psychology in the Schools* XI (1974): 191–94.

Madsen, Charles H., Jr., Wesley C. Becker, and Don R. Thomas, "Rules, Praise and Ignoring: Elements of Elementary Classroom Control," *Journal of Applied Behavior Analysis* 1 (1968): 139–50.

Madsen, Charles H., Jr., Wesley C. Becker, Don R. Thomas, Linda Koser, and Elaine Plager, "An Analysis of the Reinforcing Function of 'Sit-Down' Commands," in *Readings in Educational Psychology*, ed. Ronald K. Parker, pp. 265–78. Boston: Allyn and Bacon, 1968.

Madsen, Charles H., Jr., Clifford K. Madsen, and Don F. Driggs, "Freeing Teachers to Teach," in *Behavioral Intervention in Human Problems*, ed. Henry C. Rickard, pp. 61–75. Elmsford, N.Y.: Pergamon Press, 1971.

Madsen, Charles H., Jr., and Clifford K. Madsen, *Teaching/Discipline: A Positive Approach for Educational Development,* expanded 2nd edition for professionals. Raleigh, NC, Contemporary Publishing Company of Raleigh, Inc.

Madsen, Clifford K., "How Reinforcement Techniques Work," *Music Educators Journal* 57 (April 1971): 38–41.

Madsen, Clifford K., and Jayne M. Alley, "The Effect of Reinforcement on Attentiveness: A Comparison of Behaviorally Trained Music Therapists and Other Professionals with Implications for Competency-Based Academic Preparation," *Journal of Music Therapy* 16 (Summer 1979): 70–82.

Madsen, Clifford K., Laura G. Dorow, Randall S. Moore, and Jeana U. Womble, "Effect of Music via Television as Reinforcement for Correct Mathematics," *Journal of Research in Music Education* 24 (Summer 1976): 51–59.

Madsen, Clifford K., and John M. Geringer, "Choice of Televised Music Lessons versus Free Play in Relationship to Academic Improvement," *Journal of Music Therapy* XIII (Winter 1976): 154–62.

Madsen, Clifford K., R. Douglas Greer, and Charles H. Madsen, Jr., eds., *Research in Music Behavior: Modifying Music Behavior in the Classroom.* New York: Teachers College Press, Columbia University, 1975.

Madsen, Clifford K., and Terry Lee Kuhn, *Contemporary Music Education.* Arlington Heights, Ill.: AHM Publishing Corp., 1978.

Madsen, Clifford K., and Charles H. Madsen, Jr., *Experimental Research in Music*. Raleigh N.C.: Contemporary Publishing Co., 1978.

Madsen, Clifford K., and Charles H. Madsen, Jr., "Selection of Music Listening or Candy as a Function of Contingent versus Non-Contingent Reinforcement and Scale Singing," in *Research in Music Behavior*, eds. Clifford K. Madsen, R. Douglas Greer, and Charles H. Madsen, Jr., pp. 89–96. New York: Teachers College Press, Columbia University, 1975.

MADSEN, CLIFFORD K., and RANDALL S. MOORE, *Experimental Research in Music: Workbook in Design and Statistical Tests*. Raleigh, N.C.: Contemporary Publishing Co., 1978.

MADSEN, CLIFFORD K., RANDALL S. MOORE, MICHAEL J. WAGNER, and CORNELIA YARBROUGH, "A Comparison of Music as Reinforcement for Correct Mathematical Responses versus Music as Reinforcement for Attentiveness," *Journal of Music Therapy* XII (Summer 1975): 46–58.

MADSEN, CLIFFORD K., DAVID E. WOLFE, and CHARLES H. MADSEN, JR., "The Effect of Reinforcement and Directional Scalar Methodology on Intonational Improvement," *Council for Research in Music Education*, no. 18 (1969): 22–33.

MARHOLIN, DAVID II, and WARREN M. STEINMAN, "Stimulus Control in the Classroom as a Function of the Behavior Reinforced," *Journal of Applied Behavior Analysis* 10 (Fall 1977): 465–78.

MARTIN, FELIX, "Increasing Teachers' Positive Actions in the Classroom," *Psychological Reports* 37 (1975): 335–38.

MARTIN, GARY M. *Basic Concepts in Music*. Belmont, Calif.: Wadsworth Publishing, 1966.

MATHENY, KENNETH B., and C. RANDALL EDWARDS, "Academic Improvement Through an Experimental Classroom Management System," *Journal of School Psychology* 12 (1974): 222–32.

MONSOUR, SALLY, MARILYN COHEN, and PATRICIA LINDELL, *Rhythms in Music and Dance for Children*. Belmont, Calif.: Wadsworth Publishing Co., 1966.

MOORE, RANDALL S., "Effect of Differential Teaching Techniques on Achievement, Attitude and Teaching Skills," *Journal of Research in Music Education* 24 (Fall 1976): 129–41.

———, "The Effects of Videotaped Feedback and Self-Evaluation Forms on Teaching Skills, Musicianship, and Creativity of Prospective Elementary Teachers," *Council for Research in Music Education*, no. 47 (Summer 1976): 1–7.

MOUNTFORD, RICHARD D., "Competency-Based Teacher Education: The Controversy and a Synthesis of Related Research in Music from 1964 to 1974," *Council for Research in Music Education*, no. 46 (Spring 1976): 1–12.

MURRAY, KENNETH, "The Effect of Teacher Approval/Disapproval on Musical Performance, Attentiveness, and Attitude of High School Choruses," in *Research in Music Behavior,* ed. Clifford K. Madsen, R. Douglas Greer, and Charles H. Madsen, Jr., pp. 165–80. New York: Teachers College Press, Columbia University, 1975.

NELSON, ROSEMARY O., "An Expanded Scope for Behavior Modification in School Settings," *Journal of School Psychology* 12 (1974): 276–87.

O'LEARY, K. DANIEL, and WESLEY C. BECKER, "The Effects of the Intensity of a Teacher's Reprimands on Children's Behavior," *Journal of School Psychology* 7 (1968–69): 8–11.

O'LEARY, K. DANIEL, KENNETH F. KAUFMAN, RUTH E. KASS, and RONALD S. DRABMAN, "The Effects of Loud and Soft Reprimands on the Behavior of Disrupting Students," *Exceptional Children* 37 (1970): 145–55.

PALMER, MARY, "Relative Effectiveness of Two Approaches to Rhythm Reading for Fourth-Grade Students," *Journal of Research in Music Education* 24 (Fall 1976): 110–18.

PANTLE, JAMES E., "The Effect of Teacher Approval of Music on Music Selection and Music Verbal Preference," Paper read at Music Educators National Conference, April 1978, Chicago, Illinois.

PETZOLD, ROBERT G., *Auditory Perception of Musical Sounds by Children in the First Six Grades*. Washington. D.C.: HEW Contract, 1966.

PINKSTON, ELSIE M., NANCY M. REESE, JUDITH M. LeBLANC, and DONALD M. BAER, "Independent Control of a Pre-School Child's Aggression and Peer Interaction by Contingent Teacher Attention," *Journal of Applied Behavior Analysis* 6 (Spring 1973): 115–24.

PURVIS, JENNIE, and SALLY SAMET, *Music in Developmental Therapy*. Baltimore, Maryland: University Park Press, 1976.

RADOCY, RUDOLF E., "Effects of Authority Figure Biases on Changing Judgments of Musical Events," *Journal of Research in Music Education* 24 (Fall 1976): 119–28.

RADOCY, RUDOLF E., and J. DAVID BOYLE, *Psychological Foundations of Musical Behavior*. Springfield, Ill.: Charles C Thomas Publisher, 1979.

RAINBOW, EDWARD, "A Longitudinal Investigation of the Rhythmic Abilities of Pre-School Aged Children," *Council for Research in Music Education* (Spring 1977): 55–61.

RAPPORT, MARK D., and DARREL E. BOSTOW, "The Effects of Access to Special Activities on the Performance in Four Categories of Academic Tasks with Third-Grade Students," *Journal of Applied Behavior Analysis* 9 (Fall 1976): 372. Abstract.

REGELSKI, THOMAS A., *Principles and Problems of Music Education*. Englewood Cliffs, N.J.: Prentice-Hall, 1975.

REIMER BENNETT, *A Philosophy of Music Education*. Englewood Cliffs, N.J.: Prentice-Hall, 1970.

RINGER, V. M. J., "The Use of a 'Token Helper' in the Management of Classroom Behavior Problems and in Teacher Training," *Journal of Applied Behavior Analysis* 6 (Winter 1973): 671–77.

ROGERS-WARREN, ANN, and DONALD M. BAER, "Correspondence Between Saying and Doing: Teaching Children to Share and Praise," *Journal of Applied Behavior Analysis* 9 (Fall 1976): 335–54.

ROSS, ALLAN A., *Techniques for Beginning Conductors*. Belmont, Calif.: Wadsworth Publishing Company, 1976.

RUDOLF, MAX, *The Grammar of Conducting*. New York: G. Schirmer, 1950.

SALZBERG, RITA S., and M. AMELIA GREENWALD, "Effects of a Token System on Attentiveness and Punctuality in Two String Instrument Classes," *Journal of Music Therapy* XIV (Spring 1977): 27–38.

SANDERS, MATTHEW R., and TED GLYNN, "Functional Analysis of a Program for Training High and Low Preference Peers to Modify Disruptive Classroom Behavior," *Journal of Applied Behavior Analysis* 10 (Fall 1977): 503. Abstract.

SAUDARGAS, RICHARD W., CHARLES H. MADSEN, JR., and JOHN W. SCOTT, "Differential Effects of Fixed- and Variable-Time Feedback on Production Rates of Elementary School Children," *Journal of Applied Behavior Analysis* 10 (Winter 1977): 673–78.

SCHMITS, DONALD W., "Defining Reinforcers—A Problem in Communication for Consultation in Behavior Modification," *Journal of School Psychology* 11 (1973): 36–39.

SCHUMAKER, JEAN B., MELBOURNE F. HOVELL, and JAMES A. SHERMAN, "An Analysis of Daily Report Cards and Parent-Managed Privileges in the Improvement of Adolescents' Classroom Performance," *Journal of Applied Behavior Analysis* 10 (Fall 1977): 449–64.

SCHWADRON, ABRAHAM A., *Aesthetics: Dimensions for Music Education*. Washington, D.C.: Music Educators National Conference, 1967.

SCOTT, JOHN W., and DON BUSHELL, JR., "The Length of Teacher Contacts and Students' Off-Task Behavior," *Journal of Applied Behavior Analysis* 7 (Spring, 1974): 39–44.

SHERMAN, THOMAS M., and WILLIAM H. CORMIER, "An Investigation of the Influence of Student Behavior on Teacher Behavior," *Journal of Applied Behavior Analysis* 7 (Spring 1974): 11–21.

SIDNELL, ROBERT, *Building Instructional Programs in Music Education*. Englewood Cliffs, N.J.: Prentice-Hall, 1973.

SIMMONS, JOYCE T., and BARBARA H. WASIK, "Grouping Strategies, Peer Influence, and Free Time as Classroom Management Techniques with First- and Third-Grade Children," *Journal of School Psychology* 14 (1976): 322–32.

————, "Use of Small Group Contingencies and Special Activity Times to Manage Behavior in a First Grade Classroom," *Journal of School Psychology* 11 (1973): 228–38.

SMALL, ANN R., "Pace Yourself," *Music Educators Journal* 65 (May 1979): 30–33.

SOLOMON, ROBERT W., and ROBERT G. WAHLER, "Peer Reinforcement Control of Classroom Problem Behavior," *Journal of Applied Behavior Analysis* 6 (Spring 1973): 49–56.

SPRADLING, ROBERT L., "The Use of Positive and Negative Reinforcement in a Rehearsal Situation." Unpublished paper, Florida State University, 1969.

STANDIFER, JAMES. "Listening Is an Equal Opportunity Art," *Music Educators Journal* 56 (January, 1970): 97.

STRIEFEL, SEBASTIAN, and PAUL M. SMEETS, "TV Preference as a Technique for Selection of Reinforcers," *Psychological Reports* 35 (1974): 107–13.

STUART, MELANIE, "The Use of Videotape Recordings to Increase Teacher Trainees' Error Detection Skills," *Journal of Research in Music Education* 27 (Spring 1979): 14–19.

TALBERT, ELISABETH E., DONALD G. WILDEMANN, and MARILYN T. ERICKSON, "Teaching Nonprofessionals Three Techniques to Modify Children's Behavior," *Psychological Reports* 37 (1975): 1243–52.

TAYLOR, JACK A., "Perception of Tonality in Short Melodies," *Journal of Research in Music Education* 24 (Winter 1976): 197–208.

THOMAS, DON R., WESLEY C. BECKER, and MARIANNE ARMSTRONG, "Production and Elimination of Disruptive Classroom Behavior by Systematically Varying Teacher's Behavior," *Journal of Applied Behavior Analysis* 1 (1968): 35–45.

THOMSON, WILLIAM, "the Ensemble Director and Musical Concepts," *Music Educators Journal* 54 (May 1968): 44–46.

THORESEN, CARL E., ed., *Behavior Modification in Education: The Seventy-Second Yearbook of the National Society for the Study of Education, Part 1*. Chicago: University of Chicago Press, 1973.

TUNKS, THOMAS W., "Defining Measurable Constructs in the Affective Domain," Paper read at Southern Division Music Educators National Conference, April 1977, Atlanta, Georgia.

TURRENTINE, EDGAR M., and NEAL E. GLENN, *Introduction to Advanced Study in Music Education*, Dubuque, Iowa: William C. Brown Company, 1968.

ULRICH, ROGER, THOMAS STACHNIK, and JOHN MABRY, eds., *Control of Human Behavior, vol. III: Behavior Modification in Education*. Glenview, Ill.: Scott, Foresman, 1966.

VAN HOUTEN, RONALD, SHARON HILL, and MADELINE PARSONS, "An Analysis of a Performance Feedback System: The Effects of Timing and Feedback, Public Posting, and Praise upon Academic Performance and Peer Interaction," *Journal of Applied Behavior Analysis* 8 (Winter 1975): 449–57.

VERRASTRO, RALPH E., "Verbal Behavior Analysis as a Supervisory Technique with Student Teachers of Music," *Journal of Research in Music Education* 23 (Fall 1975): 171–85.

WAGNER, MICHAEL J., and EILEEN P. STRUL, "Comparisons of Beginning Versus Experienced Elementary Music Specialists in the Use of Teaching Time," *Journal of Research in Music Education* 27 (Summer 1979): 113–25.

WALLACE, IRVING, "Self-Control Techniques of Famous Novelists," *Journal of Applied Behavior Analysis* 10 (Fall 1977): 515–25.

WAPNICK, JOEL, "A Review of Research on Attitude and Preference," *Bulletin of the Council for Research in Music Education* (Fall 1976): 1–20.

WARNER, STEVEN P., FRANK D. MILLER, and MARK W. COHEN, "Relative Effectiveness of Teacher Attention and the 'Good Behavior Game' in Modifying Disruptive Classroom Behavior," *Journal of Applied Behavior Analysis* 10 (Winter 1977): 737. Abstract.

WHITE, MARY ALICE, "Natural Rates of Teacher Approval and Disapproval in the Classroom," *Journal of Applied Behavior Analysis* 8 (Winter 1975): 367–72.

WHITE-BLACKBURN, GEORGANNE, SUSAN SEMB, and GEORGE SEMB, "The Effects of a Good-Behavior Contract on the Classroom Behaviors of Sixth-Grade Students," *Journal of Applied Behavior Analysis* 10 (Summer 1977): 312. Abstract.

WILDMAN, ROBERT W. II, and ROBERT W. WILDMAN, "The Generalization of Behavior Modification Procedures: A Review with Special Emphasis on Classroom Applications," *Psychology in the Schools* XII (1975): 432–48.

WILLIAMS, DAVID BRIAN, "An Interim Report of a Programmatic Series on Music Inquiry Designed to Investigate Melodic Pattern Identification Ability in Children," *Council for Research in Music Education* (Spring 1977): 78–82.

WILSON, SANDRA H., and ROBERT L. WILLIAMS, "The Effects of Group Contingencies on First Graders' Academic and Social Behaviors," *Journal of School Psychology* 11 (1973): 110–17.

WINETT, RICHARD A., "Behavior Modification and Open Education," *Journal of School Psychology* 11 (1973): 207–14.

WINETT, RICHARD A., CHARLES D. BATTERSBY, and SHARON M. EDWARDS, "The Effects of Architectural Change, Individualized Instruction, and Group Contingencies on the Academic Performance and Social Behavior of Sixth Graders," *Journal of School Psychology* 13 (1974): 28–40.

WOODERSON, DAWN C. "The Effect of Musical and Non-Musical Media to Facilitate Sight-Word Learning," a paper read at the Music Educators National Conference, April 1978, Chicago, Illinois.

YARBROUGH, CORNELIA, "Competency-Based Conducting: An Exploratory Study," Proceedings of Symposium on Current Issues in Music Education, June 1978, Ohio State University, Columbus, Ohio.

———, "Effect of Magnitude of Conductor Behavior on Students in Selected Mixed Choruses," *Journal of Research in Music Education* 23 (Summer 1975): 134–46.

———, "The Effect of Videotaped Observation and Self-Evaluation on Rehearsal Behavior of Student Conductors," Paper read at Music Educators National Conference, March 1976, Atlantic City, New Jersey.

———, "A Technique for Teaching and Evaluating Basic Conducting Competencies," Paper read at Symposium on Research in Music Behavior, October 1978, Atlanta, Georgia.

YARBROUGH, CORNELIA, MARGARET CHARBONEAU, and JOEL WAPNICK, "Music as Reinforcement for Correct Math and Attending in Ability Assigned Math Classes," *Journal of Music Therapy* XIV (Summer 1977): 77–88.

YARBROUGH, CORNELIA, JOEL WAPNICK, and ROSEANNE KELLY, "The Effect of Videotape Feedback Techniques on Performance, Verbalization and Attitude of Beginning Conductors," *Journal of Research in Music Education* 27 (Summer 1979): 103–12.

YAWKEY, THOMAS D., and DAWN M. JONES, "Application of Behavior Modification to Learning Center Choices in a Kindergarten Open Education Classroom," *Psychology in the Schools* XI (1974): 321–28.

ZURCHER, WILLIAM, "A Data-Based Credit System for Performing Groups: A Third Year Report." Paper read at Symposium on Research in Music Behavior, November 1978, Atlanta, Georgia.

Index